GROUPS THAT
REVITALIZE

Available in the Replant Series

Am I a Replanter?: 30 Days of Discerning God's Call, Bob Bickford and Mark Hallock

Be a Barnabas: Helping Your Replant Be All God Wants It to Be, Mark Hallock

God's Not Done with Your Church: Finding Hope and New Life through Replanting, Mark Hallock

Groups that Revitalize: Bringing New Life to Your Church through Sermon-Based Small Groups, Kenneth Priest and Alan Stoddard

Pathways to Partnership: How You and Your Church Can Join the Replanting Movement, Bob Bickford and Mark Hallock

Raising Up Replanters: A Start-Up Guide for Your Church, Mark Hallock

Replant 101: How You Can Help Revitalize Dying Churches, Mark Hallock

Replant Roadmap: How Your Congregation Can Help Revitalize Dying Churches, Mark Hallock

Replanting Rural Churches: God's Plan and Call for the Middle of Nowhere, Matt Henslee and Kyle Bueermann

"This is my go-to book for using sermons, prayer, and sermon-based small groups to revitalize a declining church."

Daryl Eldridge, Ph.D., *President and Cofounder, Rockbridge Seminary*

"I have been involved in church revitalization in one form or another for most of my ministry. It has become my settled conviction that nothing ultimately changes the passion, thinking, or action of God's people but the Word of God applied by the Spirit of God. In this book, a pastor and a growth consultant team up to provide a much-needed biblical emphasis on revitalization through prayer and the teaching of God's Word. Read it and use it."

Ken Hemphill, Ph.D., *Founding Director of the Center for Church Planting and Revitalization, North Greenville University*

"Kenneth Priest is a seasoned church revitalizer who leads large numbers of churches in North America toward renewal. Everything is bigger in the great state of Texas, and that is true of the challenges of church plateau or decline. This new work presents a strong biblical paradigm for the need for revitalization. As Priest and Stoddard reflect on the theological role of the pastor, you will be drawn into the understanding that it is possible for you to revitalize the church you serve. This book lifts high the priority of prayer both in the life of the church revitalizer and in the life of the laymen sitting in the pew. Reading this book on church revitalization and renewal will inspire you. Following this book and doing what it challenges all of us to do will bless you. Both you and your church will be glad you began the journey that these wise church revitalizers take you. These seasoned warriors of revitalization will make you glad you began the journey to turn around your church."

Tom Cheyney, DMin, *Founder and Directional Leader, Renovate National Church Revitalization Conference; Author of* The Church Revitalizer as Change Agent

Had I been able to incorporate the key insights that Priest and Stoddard offer, I'm convinced that the road of revitalization would have been less rocky and fraught with missteps for me as a pastor as well as for the people in the pews.

Matthew McKellar, *Professor of Preaching, Southwestern Baptist Theological Seminary*

BRINGING NEW LIFE TO YOUR CHURCH THROUGH
SERMON-BASED SMALL GROUPS

GROUPS THAT REVITALIZE

KENNETH PRIEST AND ALAN STODDARD

ACOMA PRESS

Groups that Revitalize: Bringing New Life to Your Church through Sermon-Based Small Groups

Copyright © 2019 by Kenneth Priest and Alan Stoddard

Published 2019 by Acoma Press
    40 W. Littleton Blvd. Suite 210, PMB 215
    Littleton, CO 80120
    www.acomapress.org

Unless otherwise noted, all Bible references are from the ESV® Bible (The Holy Bible, English Standard Version®), copyright © 2001 by Crossway, a publishing ministry of Good News Publishers. Used by permission. All rights reserved.

Requests for information should be addressed to:

The Calvary Family of Churches
    40 W. Littleton Blvd. Suite 210, PMB 215
    Littleton, CO 80120
    www.thecalvary.org
    office@thecalvary.org

Cover Design: Evan Skelton

Interior Layout: Evan Skelton

First Printing, 2019

Printed in the United States of America

Paperback ISBN: 978-1-7336903-8-6
PDF ISBN: 978-1-7336903-9-3

TABLE OF CONTENTS

We dedicate this work to those we have encouraged to walk with Christ through the advancement of gospel work in the local church. Your commitment to healthy churches has been a blessing to us as we continue to work for the sake of Christ in all we do.

Thank you for joining us on the journey.

— KENNETH & ALAN

ACKNOWLEDGMENTS

We want to thank Judi Hayes who has been editor of this project and others we have been involved. Without her involvement, this work would not have been completed.

Additional thanks to Debbi, my wife. Her continued support and encouragement of me makes me the ministry leader I am. Also to Dr. Jim Richards and the Southern Baptists of Texas Convention where the process of sermon-based small groups in church revitalization has been an integral part of our work since 2014.

— KENNETH PRIEST

Additional thanks to Jeana for her support in ministry and her encouragement in the service to the kingdom.

Also to the churches in Texas, Arizona, and New Mexico I have served and have implemented methods in sermon-based small groups.

— ALAN STODDARD

FOREWORD

Church revitalization is a subject for which I have considerable passion. While I wasn't sharp enough to use the term "revitalization" when I accepted the pastorate of a once healthy but declining church more than thirty years ago, revitalization was exactly what it needed. The early days of this pastoral assignment were a challenge to say the least. However, through many pastoral "toils and snares," the Lord did a wonderful work of revitalization for which I had a front row seat. While I will forever be grateful for such a privilege, I can't help but wish that I might have been able to access the principles of church revitalization contained in the book you now hold in your hands. Had I been able to incorporate the key insights that Priest and Stoddard offer, I'm convinced that the road of revitalization would have been less rocky and fraught with missteps for me as a pastor as well as for the people in the pews.

I don't think I need to convince you for the need of church revitalization within our denomination. The facts speak for themselves. As the authors of this book note, in the past eighteen years Southern Baptists have not been able to reverse the declining trend within their own denomination. How may this crisis be addressed? I think this book is a good starting point. While not lengthy in terms of pages or loaded with technical jargon, it offers the reader a biblical foundation and practical perspective for church revitalization.

For example, the authors remind the pastor that revitalization is not a business endeavor but a spiritual issue. Revitalization is a spiritual issue that calls for a spiritual source-the word of God. I'm convinced that a crucial element in church revitalization is a reorientation to the sufficiency and centrality of Holy Scripture. The word was sufficient and central for the early church. Its leaders prioritized prayer and the ministry of the word (Acts 6:4). Seemingly, many church leaders and members think the word is not enough for the twenty-first century. Too often, churches resort merely to a plethora of programs and attractive initiatives to engage the culture around them. While I am not against effective programming and the quest to reach people, I believe it is useless to pack the church calendar with scintillating programs if our first "program" isn't the program of proclaiming and applying the word of God.

Next, with clarity and intentionality, the authors propose a revitalization journey that prioritizes public proclamation and personal application. Their vehicle for this journey is the sermon-based small group approach. The genius of this approach is that it effectively connects the worship service and its sermon to the small group structure of the church. It's a model that banks on the word of God, fueled by the Holy Spirit, to do what it alone can do-revitalize churches. This model also stresses the vital role of prayer. Prayer and the word were twin priorities in the early church. They should be in the church of the twenty-first century as well.

Finally, perhaps the major strength of this book is that it offers a path forward for churches of every shape and size. You don't need a big staff, a big building or a big budget. You just need a big God who has promised to do beyond all that we think or ask (Ephesians 3:20-21). Remember, He is the ultimate revitalization expert!

MATTHEW MCKELLAR

Professor of Preaching, Southwestern Baptist Theological Seminary

INTRODUCTION

All organizations have a life cycle. In addressing the life cycle of the church, some spiritual considerations must be accepted. The spiritual considerations may not be understood. God may have chosen to flourish a church in the midst of an environment where such flourishing makes no sense. This supernatural growth is at the core unexplainable. However, in general, God has established a natural order for the world and all its organisms. As such, the church functions within this natural order and adheres to natural growth patterns. Many factors create this natural growth pattern for the church: size of the building, number of core leaders, leadership style of the senior pastor, and more. These same factors can be the cause of decline in the local church. If one element is out of place or is not functioning correctly, then the church may decline. This certain reality is becoming increasingly more observable in today's church environment. In 2001, Clegg and Bird appropriately noted: "Roughly half of all churches in America did not add one new person through conversion growth last year."[2] Fifteen years later the outcome is even worse.

David Olson quotes T. S. Eliot's poem *The Rock* in his writing of *The American Church in Crisis*: "And the church must be forever building, and always decaying, and always being restored."[3] This poem provides a perfect depiction of the life cycle of the church. Olson goes on to say,

> 'Always being restored' describes a spiritual and supernatural act of God. Restoration takes place when God acts through the power of the gospel story and the movement of the Holy Spirit, breathing life into his church. The combined process of building and restoration unite human and divine efforts to fashion the house of God.[4]

Restoration for the church is more than physically restoring a building. This is the restoring of the human condition to a rightness with God that has drifted away due to a failure to submit to the authority of God's Word personally and corporately via a local church.

In 1998, Ken Hemphill stated,

> A 'Great Commission strategy'—featuring age-based Sunday schools, the revival of Sunday school as an evangelistic tool and a change of focus from style to passion—is critical to reversing the decline and plateauing of many churches today."[5]

Over the past eighteen years, Southern Baptists have not reversed the declining trend within their own denomination, which is the authors' affiliation by virtue of church membership and vocation. "The percentage of adults in the United States who attend church is decreasing."[6] This reality has not impacted Christendom enough emotionally for churches to respond. "The decline in Christianity has been going on for [more than] fifty years."[7] Even though these certainties have been articulated by leaders over the past several years, only in recent years are any attempts being made to reverse this trend. "The percentage of Americans who attend a Christian church on any given weekend declined from 20.4 percent in 1990 to 17.5 percent in 2005."[8] Much of what is being attempted is being done individually, and not much effort has focused on a strategy which equips persons for the purpose of revitalization.

"In America, it takes the combined efforts of eighty-five Christians working over an entire year to produce one convert."[9] The average Southern Baptist church in America has ninety-one regular attenders.[10] The comparative effort on this means it will take most SBC churches one year to reach just one person. "The unchurched population of the United States is the largest mission-field in the English speaking world and the fifth largest globally."[11]

"We must throw out any notion that God is truly at the center of the church's heart in North America."[12] The reality is the,

> American church is in crisis. At first glance this may not be apparent, but while many signs of its evident success and growth abound, in reality the American church is losing ground as the population continues to surge.[13]

If the biblical definition of a healthy church includes measurable outcomes demonstrating spiritual vitality, then using sermon-based small groups to reinforce a pastor's sermon will assist the pastor in deepening the principles of revitalization through the broader church body. While some members of respective churches demonstrate spiritual health and vitality, nearly 30 percent of SBC churches are in decline. Additionally, biblical spiritual health records numbers being added to the kingdom, Acts 2:42–47. Baptisms are down in SBC life, and significant kingdom advancement is not keeping up with the population growth in the United States. Therefore, not only are baptisms declining, but kingdom impact is not reaching enough unchurched people to compensate for the population growth.

Our goal in writing this book is to address this decline by using a sermon-based, small-group approach to church revitalization. This is a proven method for focusing the congregation on the direction the church should be going in fulfilling the Great Commission. We believe using this sermon-based approach can prove to be an effective Great Commission strategy for your church. Our argument is simple. The people of God need to return to the Word for God, hear from God, and obey God. Therefore, our focus is on prayer, proclamation, and gospel conversation.

Chapter 1

A BIBLICAL CASE FOR CHURCH REVITALIZATION

REVITALIZE: *verb* re·vi·tal·ize \(ˌ)rē-ˈvī-tə-ˌlīz\ to make (someone or something) active, healthy, or energetic again[14]

The number of churches affiliated with the Southern Baptist Convention which are experiencing decline causes concern for the future of reaching North America. Some of these churches have attempted to reverse this trend however. Out of the more than forty-five thousand churches affiliated with the SBC, the percent who have successfully achieved a turnaround is a small fraction of the need. The rate of decline for many churches does not allow much time for these lower numbered congregations to turn around effectively. Financial struggles are already an issue for many of these smaller churches. Add in a declining congregation, and the lack of resources makes the ability to turn around even more difficult. Whether a smaller congregation or not, as the church begins to decline, a leadership drain occurs as well. Therefore, a lack of structure is present which would permit growth. The pastors of these churches become discouraged and oftentimes experience feelings of failure.

The goal of any revitalization work should be that of personal spiritual renewal. The pastor's proclamation of God's Word to the church is to equip and encourage the church for the purposes of accomplishing the Great Commission in the church's present context. In a revitalization work the need is to establish the purpose of the church and her work and to remind the congregation of the great need that is present. After proclamation, the pastor must also provide practical application.

GOD INTENDS FOR HIS CHURCH TO GROW

Jesus gave the commission for the church to expand several times in the Gospels and Acts (Matt. 28:18–20, Acts 1:8). This is the challenge for disciples of Christ to teach others and introduce them to Jesus, giving them the opportunity to receive salvation. The intent of the Great Commission is expansion of the kingdom of God. Therefore, this is the commission to grow the church. As the body of Christ, his disciples are the church.

Simply stated, God intends for his church to grow. Additionally, Acts 2:46-47 establishes a pattern for growth occurring in the early days of the New Testament church. This pattern shows God's people exhibiting faith and spiritual practice and the Spirit moving to add daily to the numbers who worship and follow Jesus.

Matthew 28:18–20

Jesus appears to his disciples and gives them the Great Commission, his final challenge of action for his followers. He begins with his statement of authority.

> It seems, then, that Mt. 28:18 is most likely to represent a reaffirmation of authority after the rejection of Jesus by the Jerusalem authorities which led to his death. Through resurrection God has vindicated Jesus, who is now able to freshly affirm his authority.[15]

This statement of authority is also setting the stage by which the disciples would accomplish the ministry Jesus had intended for them to do. "This was critically important. Without the Messiah's authority, the mission of the disciples and our mission today would be doomed to failure."[16] Jesus's authority is empowering the disciples he leaves behind to function within the ministry he is handing off to them. At the time they have no idea about his Spirit's coming, but his words are setting the ministry stage for them to receive the Spirit, thereby fulfilling the final portion of his Commission, "I will be with you always" (v. 20).

Jesus is passing the torch to his disciples, even as he promises to be with them forever—spiritually, not physically—to empower them for future mission. Jesus can make the claim of v. 18 only if he is fully God, inasmuch as the whole universe is embraced in the authority delegated to him. And yet he is still in some sense distinct from his Heavenly Father, so that Matthew can use the divine passive in speaking of his having 'been given' this authority.[17]

In verse 19 Jesus establishes the teaching ministry he is calling his disciples to fulfill.

Matthew has already introduced the idea of being discipled in 13:52, where the imagery was of the disciples being discipled to be scribes of the kingdom and where the scribe was seen, as are the Eleven now in 28:19, as a discipling disciple.[18]

Central to this issue, the disciples are to make disciples. This is the expansion of the kingdom of God. This is the growth of the church during this present age. Until the return of Christ, the church is to grow by making disciples. The present decline of so many churches is a failure, in at least some part, to fulfill the Great Commission calling of making disciples and reaching the nations. This leads into what will be discussed later, in that if the church is to grow, it must address the three issues stated previously of returning to the Lord, listening to the Lord, and obeying the Lord. This is where growth occurs. Absence from the Lord is resulting in decline. Spiritual decline occurs first, which then causes the numerical decline as people are no longer seeking God.

The main command of Christ's commission is "make disciples" (*mathēteusate*). Too much and too little have often been made of this observation. Too much is made of it when the disciples' "going" is overly subordinated, so that Jesus' charge is to proselytize merely where one is. Matthew frequently uses "go" as an introductory circumstantial participle that is rightly translated as coordinate to the main verb—here "Go and make." Too little is made of it when all attention is centered on the command to "go," as in countless appeals for missionary candidates, so that foreign missions are elevated to a higher status of Christian service than other forms of spiritual activity. To "make disciples *of all nations*" does require many people to leave their homelands, but Jesus' main focus remains on the task of all believers to duplicate themselves wherever they may be.[19]

Jesus makes three emphatic statements regarding the issues of making disciples. First is the word *go*.

> In the context, this Greek participle is best rendered, 'when you have gone.' 'Going' is one of the three means by which to fulfill the central command to make disciples"[20]

The second statement word is *baptizing.*

> Because baptism was so closely associated with the decision of faith (cf. Acts 2:38; 8:36–38; 10:47–48), [i]t

may be best to see baptizing as Jesus' way of summarizing the evangelistic half of the disciples' ministry.[21]

Verse 20 brings the third statement, *teaching*. This is the *what* or *how* of making disciples. In Jesus's model this is the teaching ministry. The disciples are to teach others the things they have been taught. In Matthew's Jewish culture mind-set, this teaching is about a lifestyle.

> Matthew shares the general Jewish impulse to view true religion as involving a way of life and not simply a pattern of beliefs. So what is to be taught is to keep—that is, to implement in obedience—what has been commanded.[22]

Therefore once people are baptized—or evangelized—it is time to teach them the things of Jesus. Teaching "represents the other half of the disciples' ministry—the edification of those who are already believers."[23] Jesus's command to teach is a holistic command: "teach . . . all that I have commanded you" (Matt. 28:20). This command continues to this day. The believers who make up the church are to teach all they know of Jesus. Today, what is known of Jesus is taken from his Word. Therefore, we are to teach God's Word as the teaching ministry of our Great Commission strategy.

These three emphatic statements address a group of people who are supposed to be discipled in verse 19, "all nations." The call to reach the nations is evident here, though it is not to neglect a person's present context.

Matthew has already created a whole-world perspective in his Gospel prior to the present culminating mission charge. Though the claim is made from time to time, 28:19 does not turn from the Jews to the Gentiles; rather, it widens the scope from that of 10:5, which is in view. Matthew uses ἔθνη *alone* when referring to the Gentiles, but when he speaks of 'all the ἔθνη,' he no longer uses ἔθνη to distinguish Gentiles from Jews but rather refers to the whole of humanity.[24]

Acts 1:8

Prior to Jesus's ascension to heaven, he appeared to his disciples one final time. They gathered at the Mount of Olives. The disciples' mind-set was one of waiting for Jesus to establish his kingdom, now more than ever having seen the power of the resurrection. Beginning in verse 6, they ask, "Lord, will you at this time restore the kingdom of Israel?" "In Jewish thought God's promises often referred to the coming of Israel's final salvation."[25] Jesus's response to them was to set their attention in the appropriate direction prior to his leaving them.

> Verse 8 places the disciples' question in proper perspective. The 'restoration of the kingdom' involves a worldwide mission. Jesus promised the disciples two things: power and witness.[26]

The major focus on this passage is that of being global witnesses for Jesus.

> Notice that the call to witness is not limited to any select group of people since it spreads from the apostles to the 120 believers and on throughout the pages of Acts. Nor

can we restrict it only to service in our own churches or to some kind of 'professional ministry.' Every believer should be a 'world Christian,' able to function for the Savior from the other side of the street to the other side of the world.[27]

The global expansion of the kingdom of God was his intent. The church which is faithful to fulfill the Great Commission will experience growth. Growth must occur spiritually before it can occur numerically.

Acts 2:46–47

Verse 46 establishes the spiritual practices believers were involved in during the launch of the New Testament church. This text clearly lays out a path for genuine community. "They remained faithful to their Jewish worship, devoting themselves 'with one accord' in the temple."[28] The text states they were daily in the temple and daily in one another's homes. The model for revitalization for this project, though it will not specifically have the church daily in the house of worship and in one another's homes, is taking this concept and making some application. The goal is for the church to meet in worship as is regularly scheduled but in addition to add a small-group venue for the purpose of experiencing genuine community as a family of faith akin to what was experienced in the early New Testament church.

The early church was marked by faithful attendance— meeting together daily in the temple courts. They prayed, gave, ate, and rejoiced together. They practiced the presence of Jesus.[29]

This shows a model for a vibrant community of faith. The display was a further fulfillment of Great Commission living. "In Jerusalem the temple was the primary place where crowds would be found, and there the Christians went to bear their witness."[30]

Further, the home would have been seen as the place of fellowship.

> In the intimacy of the home setting, a common meal was shared together, probably including the Lord's Supper as well. It was a time marked by rejoicing in their fellowship with one another and with the Spirit and by their own openness and sincerity.[31]

The homes of the day would not have held the entire group, so we see the moving from house to house, indicating the believers exercised genuine hospitality.

> Their witness included a demonstration of hospitality. No home would be large enough to house even a small group of believers for a short time, so they literally went house to house. Luke wants us to see how good it was— they enjoyed favor with the people. Not the Sanhedrin, but common folks all around the city.[32]

Verse 47 brings the issue of growth.

> What happens to believers who worship, work, and witness for their Lord? The Lord grows the church. Let's not miss the order—first godly relationships with each other, then growth.[33]

> The growth must be seen as the outcome of obedience to the spiritual practices the early church engaged. The pure and simple life of the disciples doubtless commended them to the people, and made it easier for them to gain confidence, and so converts, but the growth of the Church, St. Luke reminds us, was not the work of any human agency . . . the work of salvation there attributed to Jehovah by the Old Testament Prophet is here the work of Christ the inference is again plain with regard to our Lord's divinity.[34]

God causes the growth when His people are focused on making disciples.

RETURN TO THE LORD

The first area of church revitalization to address biblically is to return to the Lord. A church that is experiencing a plateau or decline is going through a time of spiritual crisis. People respond to crises differently. Much of an individual's response depends on how those in the individual's circle of influence respond to assist. In relation to church growth, people at a point of crisis either grow closer to God or drift away from God. If the church (the local body of believers) does not effectively respond in crisis situations to those around them, then they most likely are not dealing with crisis effectively as a hole. The resulting elements are demonstrated through conflict and strife within the congregation. The church must first take a biblical approach to addressing the crisis. This is returning to the Lord.

Revelation 2:1–7

The writer John begins in chapter 1 with the explanation of writing this letter. The text tells us that this is the revelation of Jesus, and it was given to John by the angel of the Lord. John further recounts he is simply reporting what has been shown to him. Jesus sends word to seven churches in Revelation 2–3. Each church has a specific issue and/or word of exaltation from Jesus.

> Each of the seven letters is addressed to the angel of the church. Revelation 1:20 first mentions these angels, which are the seven "stars" in Jesus' hand in 1:16. The Greek word angelos is often translated "messenger"— whether heavenly or earthly. This sense is surely in mind here. Each letter traces the following route:

> Jesus → John → messenger → church

> Who were these messengers? The best suggestion is that they were pastors. The responsibility of pastors is to "shepherd the flock" entrusted to their care. [35]

Chapter 2 opens with an address to the church of Ephesus.

> The first arrival of the gospel in Ephesus is unrecorded. According to Acts 2.9 Jews resident in Asia were present in Jerusalem on the day of Pentecost. And we are told of 'disciples' in Ephesus before Paul's arrival, though they are represented as imperfectly instructed.[36]

What is known about Ephesus at this time is that it is a major seaport city in Asia Minor. The temple of

Artemis, one of the seven wonders of the ancient world, was found here.[37]

> Ephesus may be addressed first because it played a leading role in the beginning of the Christian church in the Gentile world (it was the center of the Pauline mission and later the residence of John). It also had geographical priority since it was the best port of entry into that part of Asia Minor.[38]

Jesus's words are used to let the church know he sees what they are doing and knows where they have been faithful. This reality is certain for the church today as it was in John's vision. Jesus is aware of his bride and how she represents him to the world.

> Christ's introduction of himself as holding the seven stars and walking among the seven golden lampstands, which refers back to ch. 1, directly relates him to the problem of the Ephesian church. He is always in their midst and therefore is keenly aware of how they are living.[39]

Verse 2 begins a threefold commendation for the church at Ephesus. They have shown themselves to be faithful in the work they were doing, deeds they had done, and not tolerating false teachings. This is illustrative of a church that is doing right and good things. They were a doctrinally sound church.

> The last sentence of verse 2 explains one aspect of the hard work of these believers: they had ejected evildoers from their church, and they had tested and rejected some false apostles.[40]

Verse 3 further shows their patience in the midst of difficult situations.

> From their earliest days as a church, these Christians had put up with hostility from those who worshiped other gods (Acts 19:23–41). They had been vigilant over the years in all the persecutions that came their way.[41]

The early church used careful examination of teachings and of behaviors of the teachers in order to determine how authentic someone was;[42] which is still a great evaluation for the church today.

Verse 4 is where Jesus lays out his concern for the church. He holds against them a failure to hold to their first love.

> The idea is that they no longer expressed their former zealous love for Jesus *by witnessing to him in the world.* This is why Christ chooses to introduce himself as he does in v 1. His statement that he 'walks in the midst of the seven golden lampstands' is intended to remind the introverted readers that their primary role in relation to their Lord should be that of a light of witness to the outside world.[43]

In the issue of church revitalization, returning to the Lord is returning to this first love. The zealous witness of Christ for Christ to the world is an imperative. The church cannot grow and will not grow when the gospel is absent. Jesus is against the church that is not evangelistic in its community. Faithfulness to doctrine is great and certainly to be praised, but faithfulness to doctrine and not to being a witness is unbiblical and not as Christ has intended.

In verse 5 Jesus calls for repentance. *Repentance* is defined as,

> the acknowledgement and condemnation of one's own sins, coupled with a turning to God. True repentance springs from love of God whom human sin rejects or offends. It includes sorrow for sin committed, confession of guilt, and the purpose of amendment. The Greek word μετάνοια, translated 'repentance' in the English NT, emphasizes the last aspect.[44]

This final aspect, the calling for amendment, is the call to action Jesus seeks. He desires the church at Ephesus to *do* something, not just feel remorseful for not doing it. This needs to be the clarion call for the plateaued and declining church today. The church must *do*, turn from not engaging in witness, and begin engaging the community for the cause of Christ.

> Christ's command to this loveless congregation was a three-pronged remedy. First, they must remember the days of their first love. They were not to live in the past, but to recall past greatness. Some no doubt resented the notion that they had fallen, but Christ considered loss of proper motive in the Christian life to be serious sin indeed. Second, they must repent of their loveless attitudes toward others. Third, they must return to the things you did at first, that is, works motivated by love for others.[45]

Failure to respond appropriately to this challenge from Jesus has dire consequences. He specifically says, "I will come to you and remove your lampstand . . . , unless you repent," (v. 5).

> Although Christ has promised to build his church worldwide (Matt. 16:18), he guarantees permanence to no individual congregation. A loveless church is no longer truly a church, and Christ has the right to extinguish such a congregation.[46]

In verse 6 Jesus returns to a word of affirmation, "the Nicolaitans taught that some degree of participation in the idolatrous culture of Ephesus was permissible."[47] The church in Ephesus, due to their doctrinal integrity, knew this was unacceptable and stood against such teachings. So, Jesus again affirms their stance on issues of false or misguided teachings.

The conclusion of the letter, verse 7, is to encourage acceptance and belief in what has previously been stated. In doing so, salvation is gained. "There is some indication that the 'tree of life' was associated with the cross of Christ in the mind of John."[48] This same outtake is relevant for the church today, "the one 'who has an ear' is the church member who both hears and heeds the message as it is read in the congregation."[49] The church must return to Jesus in order to experience renewed growth.

LISTEN TO THE LORD

The second area to address biblically in church revitalization is to listen to the Lord. The people of God must be open to hearing from him. This is accomplished by hearing from the Word of God. As the church meets throughout the week and opens God's Word, the design should be to hear from the messenger God has placed in the church, the senior pastor. The messenger shares from his time in prayer and study of God's Word. The message should be focused on the direction God is leading the local church in its context to go.

A great example of listening to the Lord is found in Nehemiah with the prophet Ezra.

> This is the first mention of Ezra in the book of Nehemiah. He had come to Jerusalem thirteen years previously, with about three thousand returning Jews (1754 males), holding a commission from Artaxerxes to appoint magistrates in Judaea. He had forced the Jews to separate from their heathen wives.[50]

In this passage the people asked him to read the Law. "Just as these people took the initiative, we should encourage all Christian believers to take the initiative in seeking spiritual revival."[51] Church revitalization will only occur when the people of God are open and seeking personal spiritual renewal for themselves.

Nehemiah 8:1–8

Verse 1 has the people of God asking Ezra to read the Law to them. This time of reading from the Torah would have been one element of synagogue practice during the Old Testament times.

Williamson has suggested that we have here almost the same elements as in a typical synagogue service: (1) the assembly of the people; (2) the request for reading of the Torah; (3) the opening of the scroll; (4) the people standing; (5) the praise (by Ezra); (6) the response of the people; (7) sermon instruction; (8) reading the law; (9) oral explanation and exhortation; (10) departure for a fellowship meal (v. 10).[52]

This same model can be expressed in the local church today: (1) the gathering of the people; (2) the desire to have the reading of God's Word; (3) the opening of the Bible; (4) the people standing (in some churches at least); (5 & 6) praise and response (pastor, worship leader, and the people); (7) sermon instruction; (8) reading of God's Word; (9) oral explanation and exhortation; (10) departure for fellowship/community.

Verse 2 gives the importance of the community's desiring to hear from God. The text states all who could understand were present and stood for reading. This meant men, women, and children.

> The Old Testament emphasizes that God's Word is to be known and used by all the people, not only the priests and leaders. Early Christians adopted this same principle. This changed as time went on as fewer and fewer people had access to the Bible. The Protestant Reformation, with its emphasis on *sola scriptura* (on the Bible as the *sole* authority for faith and practice) returned to the biblical principle that every believer should read Scripture as God's Word for their lives.[53]

The entire church must place a priority on being present to hear the Word of God proclaimed.

Verse 3 gives an idea of how long they were present standing and listening to the Torah being read.

> [F]rom daylight or an hour as early as was available. The reading must have occupied at least six hours. About one-quarter of the Pentateuch might be read in that time.[54]

The people of God listened attentively during this entire reading. "God's Word preached in the power of the Holy Spirit and with authority will command attention. The reading of God's Word brings revival."[55] Revival is essentially what is needed in a church revitalization initiative.

Verse 4 shows preparation had been made for the reading of the Torah.

> This was the prototype pulpit but may have originated during the Babylonian exile along with the beginnings of the synagogue. . . . Some think the men named here were priests; however, other references specify when they are priests or Levites. Most likely these were influential lay leaders in the community. It is important for God's people to prepare special times for seeking his will and searching his Word.[56]

In times of spiritual renewal, the people of God need to hear fresh from him. Therefore, setting aside special times to seek his will and search his Word is necessary.

Verse 5 has Ezra opening the scroll and the people standing. This shows what must have been a tradition among the people when reading the Torah. "In Neh. 9:3

we note the same tradition of standing for reading the Torah, for confession of sin, and for worship."[57]

In verse 6 Ezra begins by praising God. The people join in on his preparation to reading and express reverence for the solemn occasion.

> This verse makes clear that the respect the people had for "the book" came not because they considered it an object of veneration but because it was their word from God who deserved their praise and worship.[58]

Verses 7 and 8 show the model for not only reading God's Word but also explaining the text.

Even then Scripture needed to be explained. The Old Testament was written in the Hebrew language. Since the people had lived in a foreign country all of their lives, they had lost some of their ability to understand Hebrew. Regardless, the Levites had the job of making sure the people knew what was being said. They were helping them bridge the cultural gap between the last seventy years in Babylonia with their cultural heritage as found in Scripture. It could not have been easy. Although God's Word is authoritative for life and faith and all matters of knowing God, it frequently takes hard work to understand the message of God written in a foreign language in a distant time and place.[59]

This challenge today is presented to the pastor of the local church not only to proclaim the Word but also to explain and apply the truth within the present cultural context. A revitalization endeavor typically has a cultural gap, which must be overcome as well. The church has declined and lost relevance in the community, and the pastor is working to determine how the church can reengage and close the culture gap.

OBEY THE LORD

The third area to be addressed biblically in church revitalization is to obey the Lord. Obedience is the thing believers actually *do* to demonstrate faithfulness to Christ. Although the Great Commission passages have been examined in great detail previously, this section will draw to a close what is expressed in the text as it relates to obedience.

Matthew 28:18–20

The emphasis is on making disciples; therefore, the question of discipleship has to be, how? The answer to this is found within the text as well; it is through teaching. "The main command of Christ's commission is 'make disciples' (*mathēteusate*)."[60] The obedience of this passage is faithfulness to do so. Being on mission in one's community affords the opportunity to see this come into a reality. Believers who are faithful to share the good news of Jesus will see the fruit of the harvest occur, not every time, but faithfulness to continue to share the truth creates the opportunities when God will bless you as the instrument he uses for the harvest. The Great Commission states once the person is reached, he or she is to be discipled—or taught the things of Jesus.

This teaching ministry is being obedient to the Great Commission. It is not enough simply to reach people for Christ, but seeing them come into a growing, learning relationship is needed.

KEY QUESTIONS

1. Is your church growing, plateaued, or declining? How long has this been the trend for your church? Create a chart or graph over at least he past ten years.

2. What do the authors say are evidences in the church of decline? Which of these are evident in your church?

3. According to the authors, what is the ultimate goal of church revitalization? How does this goal differ from other church growth models? What difference does this type goal make?

4. How do you know God wants the church to grow? What are the implications of this realization for your church?

5. In the Scripture passages discussed, from a church revitalization perspective, what new insights have you gained?

Chapter 2

ON THE ROLE OF THE PASTOR AND SMALL GROUPS

The pastor and leaders should be effective disciple makers themselves.

BILL HULL, *Disciple Making Pastors*

THE PRIORITY OF THE PASTOR IN THE CHURCH

The pastor is crucial to the effectiveness of a local church to make disciples. Although other positions in the church are important and needed, the pastor is the most important because the pastor usually sets the tone for action in the church.

The Origin of the Pastor

Tracing out the position of pastor is neither easy nor clear in the Old Testament. Where did the position of pastor originate? The position could go back to the father of the Hebrew family in the list of possibilities. Fathers in Hebrew culture were responsible for discipleship in the family (Deut. 6:1–9). Elders were also a part of the patriarchal culture, but Old Testament elders were not elders in the New Testament church sense.[61] The Old Testament equivalent for the position of pastor might be found to an extent in the roles of the priests and prophets. The priests ministered in the temple. The prophets proclaimed God's message to their cultures. However, the picture does not really become clear until the New Testament.

Certain pastoral qualities were evidenced in Jesus's life. To state the official office of pastor originated with him might be an overstatement. However, Jesus modeled all the attributes of a pastor (John 10:11). Jesus spent three years mentoring and developing twelve men (Matt. 10:1–4). He modeled for them how to teach, serve, heal, and evangelize. Jesus reproduced himself in the twelve apostles.[62] He expected his followers to do the same thing (John 20:21).

The apostles modeled both negative and positive attributes. The Gospels of Matthew, Mark, Luke, and John record positive ministry accomplished by the apostles, but they also record the times when they did not get it right. For example, Judas received the same equipping from Jesus as the other apostles, yet he ended up betraying Jesus (Matt. 26:14–16). Peter also received equipping, yet he denied knowing Jesus (Matt. 26:69–75).

The book of Acts records the positive employment of Jesus's work with His disciples. Peter went from denying Jesus to proclaiming him (Acts 1–12). Peter preached Jesus boldly (Acts 2:14–36), healed the sick (Acts 3:1–10), stood up for Jesus before the religious (Acts 4:1–22), provided leadership in the Jerusalem church (Acts 2:37–47; 4:32–37), served as visionary for Jesus's message and mission (Acts 10:9–48), and even went to jail for preaching and witnessing of Jesus (Acts 12:1–5). Peter is not mentioned in Acts after chapter 12, but he leaves the scene with Herod's soldiers looking for him. He ended up in Caesarea. Tradition has his final fate in fulfillment of Jesus's prophecy of his death (John 21:18–19). Peter is one example of how all of the apostles lived out Jesus's mentoring them to be shepherds of God's people.

A major transition in the New Testament is the shift from the office of apostle to the leadership position of elder.[63] After Jesus's death, burial, resurrection, and ascension, the eleven remaining apostles replaced Judas Iscariot with Matthias (Acts 1:26). The Lord added the apostle Paul as the final apostle (Acts 9:1–18). The office of apostle probably ceased to exist in AD 45 with the institution of elders by the apostles.[64] By the time the

New Testament was being penned, "the writers assumed eldership to be a fixed, apostolic institution."[65]

The apostle Paul mentored and developed many men and women in the New Testament. The most recognizable disciple was Timothy (Acts 16:1–5). Yet many others were influenced by Paul's leadership.[66] While Paul commissioned Titus to "appoint elders in every town" (Titus 1:5), Paul also established a new precedent of leadership in new churches. New Testament churches were led and governed by a plurality of elders. Within the group of elders was usually a "primary leader of the team."[67] Support for this primary leader model comes from three things. First, the number of times the apostles' names appear in Acts as compared to the Gospels drops significantly.[68] Second, events and actions that focus on each apostle also decrease in Acts when compared with the Gospels.[69] The third evidence is Paul's leadership teams from Acts 13–27 rarely had more than two on the team.[70] Once the apostles left the scene, their disciples, known as the church fathers, often became pastors of churches. The church fathers usually used elders and deacons to lead and serve their churches spiritually.

Paul provided the foundation for this leadership position when he wrote his letter to the Ephesian church. The letter to the Ephesians was a circular letter written to many churches in Asia Minor. The word *church* in Ephesians is referring to the church as a whole, not a specific local church. That is why Paul used plural nouns in the passage below. Speaking of the Lord Jesus gifting the church, Paul wrote: "And he gave the apostles, the prophets, the evangelists, *the shepherds and teachers*, to equip the saints for the work of ministry, for building up the body of Christ, until we all attain to the unity of the faith and of the knowledge of the Son of God, to mature manhood, to the measure of the stature of the fullness of Christ" (Eph. 4:11–13, emphasis added).

The primary leader of the church was the pastor-teacher. Although a few do not agree that the phrase "shepherds and teachers" means one position,[71] most scholars interpret the two nouns as one position.[72] The ESV is the only translation that translates literally the Greek word *poiemen* as "shepherd." Most other translations use the word *pastor*. The primary leader of the local church in New Testament times was the pastor-teacher. The contemporary title for this position is teaching pastor. The origin of the position of pastor started with Jesus mentoring the apostles. The apostles instituted elders, and within the elder body was a primary leader called the pastor-teacher, or pastor.

The Qualifications of a Pastor

The witness of a pastor's life in a church and community is important to the effectiveness of the church. Because of this, God through the authors of the New Testament outlined specific qualities that would make up the character of a pastor. Character is "the combination of qualities or features that distinguishes one person . . . from another."[73] Two passages largely make up the qualifications list:

> The saying is trustworthy: If anyone aspires to the office of overseer, he desires a noble task. Therefore, an overseer must be above reproach, the husband of one wife, sober-minded, self-controlled, respectable, hospitable, able to teach, not a drunkard, not violent but gentle, not quarrelsome, not a lover of money. He must manage his own household well, with all dignity keeping his children submissive, for if someone does not know how to manage his own household, how will he care for God's church? He must not be a recent convert, or he may become puffed up with conceit and fall into the condemnation of the devil. Moreover, he must be well thought of by outsiders, so that he may not fall into disgrace, into a snare of the devil. (1 Tim. 3:1–7)

Paul also identified character qualities required of elders when he wrote to Titus:

> This is why I left you in Crete, so that you might put what remained into order, and appoint elders in every town as I directed you—if anyone is above reproach, the husband of one wife, and his children are believers and not open to the charge of debauchery or insubordination. For an overseer, as God's steward, must be above reproach. He must not be arrogant or quick-tempered or a drunkard or violent or greedy for gain, but hospitable, a lover of good, self-controlled, upright, holy, and disciplined. He must hold firm to the trustworthy word as taught, so that he may be able to give instruction in sound doctrine and also to rebuke those who contradict it. (Titus 1:5–9)

The phrase Paul used in 1 Timothy 3:2 was "above reproach." He used the phrase two times in the Titus passage above. Getz says this phrase "means a spiritual leader should have a good reputation among believers as well as unbelievers."[74] Another source stated, "It means to have nothing in one's conduct on which someone could ground a charge or accusation.[75] The phrase "above reproach" is a general idea Paul used to describe the character of the pastor in an overarching way. The Timothy and Titus lists put together look like this:[76]

ABOVE REPROACH
Continued

1 Timothy 3:1-7	Titus 1:5-9
One-Wife Husband	One-Wife Husband
Sober Minded	Disciplined
Self-Controlled	Self-Controlled
Respectable	Upright
Hospitable	Hospitable
Able to Teach	Able to Teach
Not a Drunk	Not a Drunk
Not Violent	Not Violent
Gentle	Lover of Good
Not Quarrelsome	Not Quick Tempered
Not Lover of Money	Not Greedy
House Manager	Holy
Leads Children	Lead Children
Not Recent Convert	Not Arrogant
Good Reputation	Holds to Scripture

Both of these passages give fifteen spiritual traits that an elder/pastor should possess. These spiritual character traits can be divided into a variety of areas. The main categories are: (1) inner character attitudes, (2) family directives, (3) prohibitive directives, and (4) ministry requirements. The spiritual character traits categorized look like this:[77]

INNER CHARACTER	FAMILY DIRECTIVES	PROHIBITIVE DIRECTIVES	MINISTRY REQUIREMENTS
Sober Minded	One-Wife Husband	One-Wife Husband	Hospitable
Self-Controlled	Lead Children	Not Arrogant	Able to Teach
Respectable	House Manager	Not Violent	Not Recent Convert
Gentle		Not Greedy	Hold to Scripture
Good Reputation		Not Quarrelsome	
Lover of Good		Not Lover of Money	
Upright		Not Quick-Tempered	
Holy			
Disciplined			

There are a total of twenty-three spiritual character traits not counting those that are duplicates. This list provided a definite parameter for those elders. The list served as a preventive maintenance rather than a legalistic list of commandments. These qualification lists served as the guidelines for choosing elders and pastors. Such a list clearly reveals the significance of character in the leaders' lives. Notice most of the traits deal with the inner character.

Understanding the significance requires answering a question: Why was a pastor's character so important? Paul stated in detail how pastors were to keep their integrity in check. The Pastoral Letters give lists, but when Paul was in Ephesus, he challenged the leaders and elders of Ephesus, "Pay careful attention to yourselves" (Acts 20:28). Pastoral character and integrity were to be maintained with pastoral skills. Paul's writings in Timothy and Titus related to character emphasize that character was more important than tasks and abilities. This observation leads to the question, Why?

The Purpose of the Pastor

Pastors had a responsibility not only to themselves but also to their congregations. After stating that leaders should take care of themselves, Paul also said in Ephesus, "And to all the flock, in which the Holy Spirit has made you overseers, to care for the church of God, which he obtained with his own blood" (Acts 20:28). Pastors not only had to ensure they kept themselves free from compromise of character; they were also to focus on the people God had entrusted to them. Scripture required pastors to have character that allowed kingdom influence to expand in the church and communities of the early New Testament era. Warren Wiersbe said of the pastor, "There must be nothing in his life that Satan or the unsaved can take hold of to criticize or attack the church."[78] Pastors were required not simply to be good men but to be men who lived above reproach. Pastors without exemplary character would not be able to accomplish what they were called to do. Pastors' character was to be the foundation of what they would do in ministry. Lea said, "The traits demanded of the church leaders stood in sharp contrast with the character of the false teachers."[79]

The purpose and mission of the New Testament pastor is found in three Greek terms. The three terms are often used interchangeably. Each word contributes its own unique nuance to the pastor's purpose. The Greek *presbuteros* carries the connotation of an older man or someone who is mature.[80] The word is the origin for the English *Presbyterian*. The word *episkopos* means "manager."[81] Pastors of the first churches in the first century had the responsibility of managing the church to accomplish its purpose. The word *poimano* communicates three ideas: "leading, feeding, and guarding the sheep."[82] The word literally means "shepherd" as translated in most versions as "pastor" and the ESV as "shepherd" (Eph. 4:11). Together these words constituted a job description for pastors. They were to be mature managers and leaders of their flocks. These were general directions, not detailed instructions.

The apostle Paul did identify a more specific purpose for the pastor. The Titus list ends with verse 9 saying,

> He [elder/pastor] must hold firm to the trustworthy word as taught, so that he may be able to give instruction in sound doctrine and also to rebuke those who contradict it.

The passage goes on to address false teachers. Verse 9 identifies the following ideas related to a pastor's responsibilities: (1) There is an assumption pastors were taught to "hold firm" to the Scriptures. (2) Scripture was to be taught in a way that resulted in listeners' receiving "sound doctrine." And (3) Scripture was to be used to refute those who "contradict" sound doctrine. Pastors in the first century were to confront and combat false doctrine (1 Tim 1:18–20). This not only required them to prevent false doctrine in a defensive posture but sometimes in an offensive one (1 Tim 6:11). There seems to be a correlation between the character of the pastor and the work and purpose of the pastor.

The primary purpose of pastors in Acts 6:4 reveals how they employed their tasks of management, leadership, and preaching. In context, Acts 6:1–7 is about the apostles' solving a felt need in the church that had caused a racial and social division between the Hellenists and the Hebrews. The Hellenists felt they were being prejudiced against in the distribution of the food in the church. The problem was corrected by the apostles' choosing seven leaders who were responsible for organizing the food distribution. The reason for the identification of leaders and delegation of tasks was clear. The apostles realized that "it is not right that we should give up preaching the word of God to serve tables" (Acts 6:2).

The primary task of the apostles is found in their continued response. They said, "But we will devote ourselves to prayer and to the ministry of the word" (Acts 6:4). A literal translation of this verse is this: "But we to the prayer and the ministry of the word will continue steadfastly." John Franklin points out how the word *ministry* comes after the phrase on prayer.[83] Yet there is an article before the word *prayer* in the Greek, which "creates the possibility that prayer and the word are twin ideas."[84] Franklin concluded the apostles were "declaring the two ministries they must do as church leaders were mobilizing the church to prayer and preaching/teaching the word of God."[85] The apostles ministered prayer and the Word to the church and community. They used Scripture and prayer as the foundation for the church to do work corporately that obeyed the Great Commission.

The apostle Paul's advice to Timothy frequently included instruction about teaching and preaching the Word of God. Paul advised skillful reading of the Scriptures in public (1 Tim. 4:13), the development of the spiritual gift of preaching and teaching (1 Tim. 4:14–15), precise study of Scripture that would honor God (2 Tim. 2:15), the nature of Scripture (2 Tim. 3:16–17), and the nature of preaching (2 Tim. 4:2). Timothy faced many challenges, but most of them centered on his ability to know Scripture and preach it. The preaching venue was not just a church with a pulpit and a friendly crowd. Timothy at times had to confront people in a way that upset the local community. There were counterattacks on Timothy. This is one reason Paul said, "Let no one despise you for your youth, but set the believers an example in speech, in conduct, in love, in faith, in purity" (1 Tim. 4:12). Paul encouraged Timothy to keep his character above reproach so none of his opponents would be able to diminish the message of the gospel by referring to Timothy's poor character.

The role of the New Testament pastor is found in Jesus's desire to reduplicate himself in the lives of other people. Jesus taught sinful men how to live above reproach. Those same apostles taught others how to live above reproach. Jesus knew the apostles and subsequent elders, disciples, and pastors' message of the gospel would not be taken seriously if their character was questionable or bad. The character of the early church leaders was to be above reproach so the message of the gospel would be reinforced by its bearing good fruit.

THE SMALL GROUP AS THE PLACE OF DISCIPLESHIP

Pastors were the main leaders in the New Testament churches. As stated previously, the main purpose of a pastor is to preach the Word of God. The purpose of preaching is for people to be transformed into the image of Jesus Christ. Preaching should result in changed lives.[86] Is transformation so simple? Was transformation in believers in the New Testament cultivated? Where did it happen? How was it done?

The Role of the Family in the Discipleship Process

In Jewish culture the family played a great role in discipleship process. The family was led by the father. He was responsible to ensure the family followed God's commandments. Deuteronomy 6:4–9 says,

> Hear, O Israel: The Lord our God, the Lord is one. You shall love the Lord your God with all your heart and with all your soul and with all your might. And these words that I command you today shall be on your heart. You shall teach them diligently to your children, and shall talk of them when your sit in your house, and when your walk by the way, and when you lie down, and when you rise. You shall bind them as a sign on your hand and they shall be as frontlets between your eyes. You shall write them on the doorposts of your house and on your gates.

The principle of disciple making in the family and home is evident in Scripture. The Jews of the New Testament had this principle ingrained deeply in their culture. Disciple making was a way of life in Jewish culture. At its most basic level, disciple making happened in the most communal of settings, the home. The principle of casual, lifestyle disciple making was the natural example Jesus and the apostles displayed.

Jesus's Use of Small Groups

Jesus was raised in a Jewish home. Although the Son of God, he was taught Scripture and morals from Joseph and Mary (Luke 2:39–40). Jesus knew how to disciple others because (1) he was God, (2) he received instruction in the home, and (3) he led a small group to reproduce themselves. Robert Coleman points out the,

> total number of devoted followers at the end of his earthly ministry numbered little more than the five hundred brethren to whom Jesus appeared after the resurrection.[87]

Jesus came on the scene and ministered to the masses, began to look for disciples, chose twelve apostles, had three leaders among the twelve, culminated with the five hundred, and ended up with 120 followers in the Acts 1–2 prayer meeting.[88] Jesus knew the dynamics of small-group leadership. Most of Jesus's discipling and developing came when he was in a small-group setting, not large groups. Jesus taught as he lived with his disciples.[89] The small-group process was the system Jesus used not only to model evangelism to the disciples but to minister to them as well. Their equipping in those short three years changed them and prepared them to help others follow Jesus also.

The Development of Small Groups in the New Testament

Spiritual growth often happened in small groups in the New Testament. Jesus led a small group of twelve for three years. His followers followed his example. The pattern for gathering in the New Testament after the resurrection is found in Acts 2:46: "And day by day, attending the temple together and breaking bread in their homes." Temple participation was the large group. Meetings in homes represent the small group. In the book of Acts, the word "house" is used eighteen times in relation to the place where the church gathered (Acts 1:13; 2:2, 46; 5:42; 8:3; 9:17, 36; 10:6, 9; 12:12; 16:34, 40; 17:5; 18:7; 20:20; 21:8, 16; and 28:30). There are more uses of "house," but only eighteen refer to the intimate setting of the home where discipleship took place. In Paul's letters there are five uses of "house" referring to a place of gathering for the church (Rom. 16:5; 1 Cor. 16:9, 19; Col. 4:15; and Phlm 2). Second John 10 also references the church in a house.

New Testament churches were located in homes.[90] The number of churches is not given in Scripture, but the number of believers was in the thousands.[91] The thousands of believers were assimilated in the church through small groups. The leaders of these small groups were usually elders.[92] The small groups that met in houses accomplished the purposes of the church and the Great Commission.[93] Small groups were the place where knowledge of Scripture was provided and applied in believers' lives.

Since churches were in homes, the main message of the pastor was delivered there.[94] Preaching may have, at times, been more of a dialogue than a monologue.[95]

Questions and answers were a means of applying what Scripture taught. At times all believers took part in exhorting one another from Scripture (Col. 3:16). House churches were the places where people developed relationships.[96] Needs were met in a natural, nonprogrammatic way. People were in such close proximity to one another, no need could go unnoticed and unmet. The house church was not only a teaching center but also a place where pastoral care was done. Disciple making in the early church happened in the home, not in the temple.

Extending the Message in Acts

In the early church the main leader was the pastor. The pastor's message and ministry were important for the church to accomplish its mission. The pastor, being such a high priority leader, had to live his life above approach. A pastor whose character honored God was respected and heard by his listeners. Christians in the church met in homes for transformational times of discipleship. The last questions to consider theologically are: What was the method and model of content delivery in the book of Acts? Is there a correlation between the public messages preached in Acts? And what happened after the message in the homes of the Christians in Acts?

The book of Acts records principles that demonstrate there was a direct link between the public proclamation of the gospel and the personal application in smaller groups after the message. In the book of Acts, proclamation happened in two ways: proclamation was demonstrated through the preaching of the gospel and power healings.

Acts records eight examples where proclamation took place in a public place or large crowds and then was explained further or applied after the message in a smaller group. Below is a list of the examples. The first list gives direct examples. The second list provides indirect examples. Below both lists is an expanded explanation of the examples. One example in the Gospels is provided to show how Jesus used this method at times with his disciples. Another example connects the Gospels with Acts.

Five passages directly give biblical support for the use of small groups who studied and applied a previously preached message.

PERSON	PUBLIC PROCLAMATION	PERSONAL APPLICATION
Jesus	Luke 8:4–8 *Parable of the Sower*	Luke 8:9-15 *Parable Explained*
Jesus	Matthew 6:33 *Kingdom Assignment*	Acts 1:3-4, 8 *Assignment Explained*
Peter	Acts 2:14–36 *Pentecost Sermon* *Scripture after Worship*	Acts 2:37–47 *Response and Application* *of Sermon*
Philip	Acts 8:26–28 *Ethiopian Reading* *Scripture after Worship*	Acts 8:29–40 *Philip Explains Text,* *Ethiopian Saved and* *Baptized*

Paul/Silas	Acts 17:10 *Preaching in Berea*	Acts 17:11–15 *Examination of Preaching*

An examination of the details helps bring the public proclamation and personal application into view more clearly. Jesus spoke the parable of the sower in a crowd of listeners in Luke 8:4–8. He afterward took his followers, the disciples, aside to explain only to them the meaning and application of the parable.

Jesus also spoke the Sermon on the Mount in Matthew 5–7 in a large crowd. He specifically told his followers to "seek first the kingdom of God" (Matt. 6:33). He often spoke of the kingdom of God in the Gospels. After his resurrection Jesus spent forty days explaining the kingdom to the apostles in Acts 1:3–4, 8.

In Acts 2:14–36, Peter preached his first sermon at Pentecost. The purpose of the sermon was evangelistic; and the main idea, found in verse 36, conveys the priority that Jesus, whom they crucified, was both Lord and Christ. After preaching to the crowd, some within the crowd said, "Brothers, what shall we do?" (v. 37). Peter then said, "With many other words . . . continued to exhort them" (v. 40). The application of the sermon came when the respondents were baptized and assimilated into the biblical community (Acts 2:32–47).

In Acts 8:26–28, an Ethiopian eunuch was trying to understand what he heard in the worship service he had just attended. He was pondering Isaiah 53:7–8. His public experience was still influencing him after he left worship. In Acts 8:29–40, God set up a divine appointment for the eunuch. Philip the evangelist followed God's leading by going to Gaza to meet with the eunuch. Upon arrival Philip explained the text the eunuch heard in worship. The eunuch professed Christ as his Savior and was baptized.

Acts 17:10–15 records one of the most direct examples of a sermon idea being studied and applied in a smaller group afterward. In verse 10, Paul and Silas went into a Berean synagogue. Obviously, some kind of preaching or teaching happened. After the message given in the synagogue, verse 11 states, "They [the Bereans] received the word with all eagerness, examining the Scriptures daily to see if these things were so." The results were people professing Christ as Savior. It also caused trouble with those who did not believe. This encounter still mobilized the church to strategize where to make disciples next (vv. 1–15).

There are four indirect examples of where the principle of small-group discipleship is present after a preaching encounter. These examples are not as influential but are beneficial to the study of small groups and biblical discipleship.

PERSON	PUBLIC PROCLAMATION	PERSONAL APPLICATION
Paul	Acts 13:13–41 *Sermon at Antioch Pisidia*	Acts 13:42–43 *Jews and Devout Converts Receive Explanation of Sermon*

Paul	Acts 18:5–6 *Evangelistic Preaching in Synagogue*	Acts 18:7–11 *Follow-Up, Discipleship in House Next to Synagogue*
Apollos	Acts 18:24–26a *Preaching in Ephesus*	Acts 18:26b–28 *Aquilla/Priscilla Explain More Accurately*
Paul	Acts 19:8 *Preaching in Synagogue*	Acts 19:9–10 *Application in Hall of Tyrannas*

Acts 13:13–41 records a sermon Paul preached at Antioch Pidisia. The purpose of the sermon was to exhort Jews to consider the claims of Christ's being the Messiah as true (vv. 36–41). After the message the people asked that "these things" (v. 42) be proclaimed to them again. Paul and Barnabas spent more time with those who wanted answers about what they had heard (vv. 42–43).

In Acts 18:5–6, Paul preached an evangelistic message in a synagogue at Corinth. The message was not well received. Paul left that synagogue saying, "Your blood be on your own heads. I am innocent. From now on I will go to the Gentiles" (v. 6). As he left, he went to the home of a man named Titius Justus whose house was next to the synagogue (v. 7). Crispus, who heard Paul's message in the synagogue, became a believer (v. 8). Others believed and were baptized (v. 8). Paul stayed there for a year and a half developing these new believers.

Acts 18:24a–26a tells of Apollos's preaching eloquently in Ephesus. Apollos was a good communicator of the Scriptures. His weakness was that his message was somewhat incomplete because "he knew only the baptism of John" (v. 25). After the message Pricilla and Aquilla, having noticed something was missing in his message, took him aside and "explained to him the way of God more accurately" (v. 26).

In Acts 19:8, Paul preached at Ephesus for three months. The content of the message was the kingdom of God. Some at the synagogue became irritated with Paul and his message. Paul left that synagogue only to take some of his disciples with him to the hall of Tyannas. Paul stayed there two years developing and applying the message of the gospel with the people in the church (vv. 9–10).

The book of Acts clearly reveals a pattern of public proclamation that, at times, resurfaces in smaller groups after the message. The proclamation was sometimes preaching and at other times a power-healing encounter. The message was extended into people's lives for further explanation and application in various ways. The amount of time the smaller, more personal application took place varied also. Sometimes it lasted a few days, and at other times it lasted for up to two years. The basic fact is that, at times, a proclamation idea would be the idea that surfaced later for personal discipleship in believers' and nonbelievers' lives.

Implications for Contemporary Discipleship Approaches

A purpose extends like a thread from Jesus Christ to the contemporary pastor. Jesus Christ last command to His disciples was for them to "make disciples" (Matt. 28:19). A disciple is first a person who has made a decision to receive Jesus Christ as his or her Savior and Lord. Upon receiving Christ as Savior, the new believer is baptized. After baptism the new believer is expected to join a faith community, the church, to learn how to observe or do the things Jesus desires him or her to do (Matt. 28:19–20). Jesus Christ wanted and still wants his followers to be transformed. The transformation or discipleship process is not complete until a new believer can teach another new believer what he or she was taught. Jesus's desire for his followers was for their transformation to be reproduced in others.

Pastors need to lead in the discipleship process. Daryl Eldridge once said,

> Pastors should have to lead and reproduce a small group before assuming a position as pastor of a local church. Approximately 90–95 percent of pastors are not a part of a small peer group that studies the Word. They teach by their lack of involvement that small groups are not important.[97]

The pastor of the church is the one person who must model discipleship. As the main disciple the pastor's character needs to be above reproach, or the ability to preach and teach effectively is diminished. Real discipleship is not likely to take place under the leadership of a pastor whose character cannot be trusted by the congregation and community.

Twenty-one centuries after the New Testament was penned, the challenges of character, preaching, and witness are still present. Contemporary personalities like Jim and Tammy Fay Baker, Jimmy Swaggert, Henry Lyons, Ted Haggard, and Darrel Gilyard[98] compromised the impact of the message of the gospel not by their inadequate leadership and preaching ability but by their failed ability to live above reproach. The church cannot afford to see any more pastors ruin congregations and communities by their lack of character. The pastor's message is too important for the message to be unheard because of character issues. A pastor's character cannot be separated from the preaching ministry.

The main purpose of a pastor is to make disciples through preaching the Word of God for the purpose of seeing listeners' lives transformed. The New Testament reveals how the messages of pastors were communicated and applied in small house churches. The message was complemented with the pastoral care system of the small group. Pastors are the main motivators and leaders who get the gospel out to the world. Although others who are not pastors share the gospel, pastors in their preaching are the ones who ignite the fires of discipleship and transformation in others. The pastor's voice and message are crucial to the effectiveness of the spreading of the gospel to those who are not believers and the discipleship of believers.

The best place for application of the sermon today is in the small group. The practice is biblical and practical. But what would that process look like? Is anyone doing it? How would it be done? What are the benefits for pastors and churches today? These questions will orient our probe into churches that are using sermon-based small groups to produce disciples and shepherd the church.

KEY QUESTIONS

1.   Why is the pastor's role in church revitalization so significant?

2.   In what specific ways did Jesus model the role of pastor? Which of these is an area in which you would like to grow?

3.   Can the list of pastor/elder qualifications in 1–2 Timothy and Titus be derived from Jesus's example? Explain.

4.   Why does a pastor's character matter as he seeks to lead a church to revitalization?

5.   Where in your church do you see discipleship that leads to transformation? Describe this discipleship.

6.   How are proclamation and discipleship connected in your church?

7.   When is the discipleship process complete? Based on this definition, who in your church are mature disciples?

8.   If you could add to disciple making component in the church you serve, what would you add?

Chapter 3

THE PRIORITY OF PRAYER IN REVITALIZATION

There is a huge movement for the revitalization of churches today. Books, blogs, articles, and more books have been written. There is no shortage of resources to tell you how to revitalize or be an agent of revitalization in your church. When Kenneth suggested we put together a book on revitalization, I told him we needed the chapter that no one seems to include in revitalization—the chapter on prayer. The first step in revitalization is prayer. A few people will tell you this, but most will not. Recent resources on revitalization give much strategy and assumed prayer. We suggest a plan that depends on prayer. Ramping up a revitalization campaign requires prayer in the planning stage (the return stage). Prayer is crucial in the implementation.

Prayer is crucial and here is why: the church I (Alan) serve went through a split five years ago. Then for the first two to three years, we just seemed never to get to a season of health. I say that not because we were not growing numerically. The reality was that we were relationally unhealthy. Part of this is my fault. I failed to mobilize key people and the church to pray. When people pray together, they tend to become more relationally healthy. In revitalization, doing the things that bring life back to a church challenges people. Health is revealed at the challenge point. Many leaders jump to the assessments and procedures; however, we are convinced not enough praying has gone into the preparation. When the hard stuff of revitalization is addressed, people operate either with limited wisdom, fleshly wisdom, or wisdom from the business world. The wisdom of God is needed to walk through a revitalization process.

We address revitalization because most churches are at a plateau. They are not growing or declining but are on the verge of decline. No offense to others who are addressing revitalization of churches, but something is missing. What is it? Prayer. Why are we not seeing more revitalization of churches with all the resources we are producing? We make the case here that revitalization must include a real prayer plan that at least includes the leaders of the church. Loyal members who desire revival in the church should be included also.

What is revitalization? Revitalization is bringing life to something on the verge of death. It is making something once vital, vital again. What would a church look like that was revitalized? More numbers? Better health? Remember what was stated before: spiritual health precedes numerical increase. Any measurement of church health surely would start with the book of Acts. What role did prayer play in the early church? We argue from Scripture a prayer priority in Acts. We remind anyone tackling revitalization of a local church, Acts 1:8 power comes from Acts 1:4 praying. What's the priority? Look to these verses: Acts 1:4, 8, 14; 2:1, 42; 3:1; 4:31; 6:4; 7:60; 12:5; 13:3; 14:23; 16:13, 16, 25; 20:36; 27:35.

The topic of prayer is spread pretty evenly throughout Acts. Early in Acts we see a priority of prayer established in Acts 1–6. Acts 2 is the foundational passage most church leaders use to show what a church should be doing, but prayer often fails to make it on the list. It gets swallowed up in worship. The early church prayed. We believe much more prayer happened than Acts records. We would argue prayer is established in Acts 1–6 as a priority, and in Acts 7–28 it was a natural practice. While Acts 2 is the main chapter for prayer and Pentecost, Acts 6:4 is actually the anchor verse. The apostles drilled prayer down into the church as a priority not only for them but for the entire church.[99]

Most churches in need of revitalization rush to the things that bring numerical growth but forget to sow the things that guarantee a harvest that will last. Prayer paves the way. Prayer changes culture. Pray gets the church body desiring revitalization. Now one thing needs to be clarified. When we say "get your church to praying," we do not mean "pray and do nothing." Strategy is important. What we are saying is strategy is born from prayer.

WHY THE HARD PUSH FOR PRAYER?

1. Prayer kept the church unified.
2. Prayer acquired the power of God.
3. Prayer fills the church with the Holy Spirit

The same thing that happened in the first century can happen in the twenty-first century.

"PASTOR, WHEN DID WE START PRAYING?"

I (Alan) had a deacon who asked me, "Pastor, when was it you started focusing us on prayer?" I was excited someone not only noticed the change but was willing to voice the change. It was obvious. Our church culture had changed. Things were better. Better from what, you might ask. That leads to more "why the hard push for prayer." Let me give you a list.

- Those two or three men in the church who are more fleshly than spiritual.

- That little critical rumbling that never seems to go away.

- Those two to three critics in every key area you want to see revitalized.

- The tone set by your mediocre tithes and offerings that keeps things stirred up.

- Those classes that are entrenched inward at the expense of an outward focus.

- The spiritual vibrancy that seems to be missing from your worship service.

- How will you deal with the negatives that are always barriers?

If you start with strategy and procedure, you may be doomed. What happens is leaders start with strategy at a fast pace that leaves behind preparation in prayer. At the same time, leaders who do not pray are given a voice at the table of revitalization. When this happens, some at the table will treat revitalization as a business endeavor instead of a spiritual issue.

WHEN DID WE START PRAYING?

About a year from when the deacon asked me when we had started praying, I focused the church on praying after I preached Matthew 9:35–39. The Greek word in verse 37 is deomai. It means "beg or ask." Literally it means, "Ask like a beggar because we are desperate." A desire for revitalization should come from desperation that churches are not healthy and growing. One of the challenges, the main one, is creating a culture for revitalization that sticks. God prompted me to get our church body praying. Why?

When a pastor sees the church as desperate, he looks for solutions. He, as well as other leaders, wants the church to flourish in Great Commission work. So, a pastor will lead change. A meeting will be called. Then a series of meetings happens. Yet the soil will not be tilled with prayer. So, in the revitalization meetings an obligatory prayer will be offered at the start of the meeting. Once the pontificating of expertise is over (a little facetious here but not far off), another prayer will be offered asking God's blessing. The problem with this approach is that is lacks real praying that gets people involved at a spiritual level. I take a risk in saying this. Usually a church meeting can get by without prayer, which is sad. Revitalization requires a deeper, more passionate prayer. Why?

When revitalization meetings happen, they involve evaluation, and these meetings open the doors for carnal people to cause trouble. Many pastors have been sacrificed on the altar of strategizing before leading a season of praying. The amazing fact is no church growth books on revitalizing say this truth. Why? It is easier to have the expert come for $3,000 than to get before the face of God and get instructions from him. Now do not take that statement wrong. We are not saying a voice from outside the church is not good. It is good. Yet the pastor of a church will have to own revitalization at some point. The pastor should start revitalization with prayer. Prayer should permeate the entire process. As a matter of fact, revitalization should insert prayer in the center of the church. Revitalization should make a church prayer driven.

We know what you are saying now. "How do I do that?" Look at the Appendix. We are giving you a one-page plan for the average church. It is not perfect. You will need to evaluate your own church and make your own contextualized list. Yet we do believe this one page can change your church. It may take a year, six months, or ninety days. The Spirit of God will lead you if you are willing. Use the page in the appendix called "Remember the Prayers!" to start your revitalization process.

KEY QUESTIONS

1.   At what points in the revitalization process is prayer essential? How might this be implemented in your church?

2.   How can prayer lead to a passion for revitalization?

Chapter 4

CONNECTING THE SERMON TO THE SMALL GROUP

New wine is put into new wineskins.

JESUS, *Mark 2:22*

A NEW MODEL FOR DISCIPLESHIP

Every church generation has the same task: to make disciples. In contemporary times churches have used a variety of methods and programs. Of course, all churches gather for worship. In addition to the worship experience, most churches in America use either an on-campus Sunday school or an off-campus small-group system for disciple making, ministry, and evangelism. A few churches use neither a Sunday school nor a small-group system. Some offer special discipleship classes.

Acts 2:42–47 has become the paradigm passage many pastors and church leaders have used as a guide for Christian development. A sense of connectedness around the Word of God that produces ministry and missions is what seems to be missing. Many pastors have realized the biggest challenge in the church is closing the "back door of the church." The back door of the church is the idea many people enter the church as a visitor or member but fail to stick around long enough to become a developing disciple. The back door of the church in wide open and needs to be shut.[100]

A possible option for effective discipleship is one that connects the best of Sunday school and small groups.[101] Most Sunday schools focus on teaching the Scriptures. They attempt to accomplish relationship building and ministry, but the main focus is on the lesson each week. Lessons usually come from a curriculum written by a denominational agency or Christian literature business. Small groups tend to focus on relationship building and ministry. Teaching is also a component, but teaching is on the same level as relationship building and ministry. Does there have to be such a division of style between the Sunday school and small-group models? Another possible option connects the best teaching, reaching, and ministry principles of Sunday school and small groups. Sermon-based small groups provide an option to connect the worship service and sermon to small groups.

BEST PRACTICES OF SERMON-BASED SMALL-GROUP CHURCHES

The use of the sermon-based small groups (SBSG) for making disciples is a fairly new phenomenon in Western church culture. The principle of resurfacing of a biblical idea after it has been communicated goes back to the New Testament with Jesus taking his disciples aside to further explain a parable. The church in Acts, at times, followed the same pattern.

Practice #1: Involve the Senior Pastor first.

In the churches that use the SBSG approach, the senior pastor is the key player. He was bought into the process of making disciples in small groups and saw the significance of using the SBSG approach. Some churches in the surveys said the senior pastor needed to have buy-in before a staff and church could move forward in the process of implementing a SBSG model. This buy-in avoids personality and control challenges among church leaders.

In churches that use the SBSG approach, the senior pastor is involved personally in a small group. The pastor does not set up a program or an opportunity he does not take part in himself. The pastor's personal participation gives credibility to the most important process in a church: disciple making.

In churches that use the SBSG approach, the senior pastor is involved in the discipleship of other leaders. There are times when the senior pastor is not the main leader of the SBSG leaders. Other executive pastor-level leaders may lead the small-group leaders. The best churches minister to the leaders consistently and closely so the small-group leaders are healthy and can reproduce.

Practice #2: Emphasize the relationship factor.

Churches that use the SBSG approach make a philosophy shift from prioritizing content to prioritizing relationship building. These churches see discipleship as a process rather than a program. Discipleship is a part of a process of living life close enough to a few other people to make a difference in their lives. In order to emphasize the relationship factor properly, these churches keep the small groups between twelve and fourteen participants. This number allows groups to be large enough to allow some anonymity and small enough to be intimate.

Practice#3: Shift to a lecture-lab model.

The lecture-lab model shifts the main teaching or preaching event to the worship service and places the application of the message in the small group. The lecture is the preaching. The lab is the place of application. The lecture-lab model requires good preaching week by week. Since small groups are the place of relationship building and application of the sermon, the preaching before the small-group meeting must be strong.

The lecture-lab model is a master-teacher approach. The senior pastor, or others on a teaching team, becomes the main teacher in the church. The lecture-lab model does not change the topic from Sunday to when the small group meets. The topic from the Sunday message is the topic in the small group. Weak preaching with little content from Scripture will leave the participants with little to apply. With the lecture-lab model small groups do not have teachers but leaders, shepherds, and facilitators. These positions require mature people who are able to lead a group to grasp a church's and small groups' vision. The small-group leaders must be taught how to lead small groups and reproduce them. The leaders are able to reproduce a group by apprenticing their replacements. The leaders cast a vision to their groups to birth a new group at some point. The positions require people not to teach but to pastor and serve the people in the group. They also require someone who can lead a discussion with skill and at times know how to react to things that are unplanned by the SBSG material.

Practice #4: Implement the plan strategically.

Churches that use the SBSG approach strategically plan for the process to be successful and a win without disrupting the equilibrium of the church. Most of the churches surveyed were established churches. If a new church start were to implement the SBSG model, the process might be easier. Most of the churches using the SBSG model did not require the approach to be used by everyone. The model was offered as an option. Any pastor wanting to start this type of small-group approach should count the cost. The pastor should start slow and small. Before starting, do the research by examining the models and designing one that fits your own church culture and community. Handpick the first leaders and get them to enlist their own friends to start the first group. A good start with a plan for reproduction will help avoid mistakes and enhance the possibility of success.

Practice #5: Follow a "simple-church" approach.

Churches that use the SBSG model keep other programming simple. Other events are strategic and minimal. The main ministry venue is the small group. Churches using the SBSG model do not pack their church calendars with busy events that compete with the SBSG slot. The SBSG model challenges pastors to sign off on the two-slot motif. The first slot is the Sunday morning time slot, the church's worship service. The second slot is the slot that many church members will give outside of Sunday morning. SBSG church fills the second slot with a small-group participation opportunity. SBSG churches know few members will give up a third time slot.

Practice #6: Utilize a website effectively.

The churches that best use the SBSG approach use their church websites to communicate. The church communicates the preaching series which usually has an engaging, motivating, or felt-need title. The series promotion is on the home page, or there is a clearly visible link to the message page. The message page includes a user-friendly page linking members to an opportunity to download recent messages by podcast, mp3, or video using UStream, Youtube, or Vimeo options. Video messages are imbedded into the page. The message page also provides SBSG materials in pdf form. The effective use of a website can create a culture that encourages members to listen to the message even if they are not physically on campus. Also, the strongest churches have leadership development and leader communication. Some churches turned in attendance records online. Cutting-edge SBSG churches value time and use their website to maximize it.

Practice #7: Design engaging curriculum.

SBSG churches design small-group material that appeals to the eye, head, and heart of participants. The material looks inviting. Cutting-edge churches have SBSG material that looks contemporary while not being expensive to produce. The material includes a little color in the church's logo and usually matches the website design. The look of the material is such that it could be viewed as trendy or catchy.

The material could fit in a Bible easily without being cumbersome. The material is portable not only to a person's devotional life and small group but also the marketplace. SBSG churches develop material that is discussion oriented. It appeals to the heart with engaging content based on the Sunday sermon. Most churches design the material to be completed before the group meets. A few other churches do not require homework at all. SBSG churches reach the heart of participants through ministry projects and mission trips.

Practice #8: Connect the vision statement to the discipleship process.

Cutting-edge churches using the SBSG model include their vision statement on the material. The vision statement is an expression of the church's discipleship process. When participants receive the SBSG material, they see the vision statement as part of what they are doing by participating in small group. These churches seem to have a higher level of commitment to the SBSG model as the way to do discipleship in place of other programs.

Practice #9: Offer off-campus groups.

Most SBSG churches use off-campus groups that meet after the sermon is preached. Churches use various names for groups such as growth groups, sermon-based home fellowships, small groups, or life groups. SBSG churches use a living room over a classroom on campus because of the intimate atmosphere a living room provides. Since relationship building is a primary core value, homes seem best for these groups to create long-term, significant relationships.

Practice #10: Offer Sunday School options.

Some churches use the SBSG model use it in a Sunday school format. Sunday school models vary in curriculum design. One strength in using the Sunday school model is it allows participants to use on-campus rooms and child-care options. The Sunday school option is used by a minimal percentage of the church's total groups.

Practice #11: Equip groups to provide pastoral care.

Churches that use the SBSG model develop a culture within the group where pastoral care is provided from the group. The traditional paradigm for pastoral care is that paid staff go to the hospital, visit the sick, and counsel church members. SBSG churches make the decision to expect small-group leaders to provide pastoral care. This standard is communicated to members, and they receive it. This is a part of the DNA of the church. This lightens the load on staff members. It expands the circle of ministry. Leaders are healthier because they serve as lay pastors. Members are healthier because more are served because churches have more lay leaders than the paid staff members.

Practice #12: Conduct ministry/missions projects in groups

Questions in the material are focused not only on personal life issues but also on doing ministry in the community and world. The SBSG model pushes groups to do ministry from within their groups and do not view ministry opportunities separately. The projects and trips are posted on the SBSG material so they are always visible. Ministry and missions are intentional in SBSG churches. Most opportunities for ministry and missions are funneled through the SBSG at least annually and preferably biannually.

PRINCIPLES FOR WRITING
DISCUSSION-BASED MATERIAL

Principle #1: Collaborate in sermon preparation.

Writing SBSG material starts with sermon preparation. Sermon collaboration within the staff team is beneficial.

Churches that use the SBSG model best are those that plan out a preaching series months ahead of time. The series is branded with a felt need in mind. Creativity is deeper and wider if more people are involved. Allowing other staff members or teaching pastors to participate in sermon preparation gives them buy-in. Ministers of prayer, discipleship, spiritual formation, as well as media experts, can bring many needed angles to the Sunday morning worship experience. These cutting-edge churches meet for a preaching preparation retreat twice a year. The staff meets weekly after the six-month plan has been developed to fill in the details. The preaching pastor shares the preparation process while retaining the right to make final decisions. The preaching pastor still brings his own unique personality to the message.

Principle #2: Form a writing team.

Developing SBSG material varies from church to church. A common method among the churches that have excellent material is that they use a writing team. Use of a writing team relieves the pressure on one person having to do it. A rotating team is one approach that works. This prevents burnout and allows for writers to have downtime for spiritual growth related to creativity. It also allows for professional growth in writing discussion questions. Another option is to have the team meeting on a weekly or monthly basis to write questions in collaboration with the sermon preparation team. A few pastors write the SBSG discussion questions directly from their sermon notes.

Principle # 3: Maintain an application focus.

SBSG churches focus on applying the Sunday morning message in small-group material. Knowledge and understanding questions are present in the material, but the strongest focus is on doing the Word. Application is surfaced through questions designed to bring the text to daily life. SBSG churches set up an atmosphere for transformation by reinforcing biblical truths and challenging participants to see the message extended into their lives. Discussion is desired over lecture. The lecture, or sermon, has already provided the content of the small group. The group afterward applies the text. Application happens in personal life examination and through ministry projects the group does together.

Principle #4: Choose a writing model.

SBSG churches use a variety of writing models to develop curriculum. The churches that seem to be the strongest use a template. The template outline helps the writing process. A template allows the writer or writing team to know beforehand what type of questions need to be written and how many questions are needed for each category in the template. A template makes delivery to small-group participants easier. It streamlines the learning process. Small-group participants know beforehand what the template looks like. They become familiar with it. The template encourages participants to participate and helps them grow spiritually by narrowing the focus for them.

Other SBSG churches use a more flexible approach when writing curriculum. Another approach is brainstorming ideas and angles for questions around the text or the sermon's big idea. The writing process is less precise. Some churches use a couple of the same questions each week. These one or two questions get participants to listen closely to the sermon and identify what is liked most or what is the most challenging. Churches that do this then use two to three other questions related to the text but focused on what the participant will do in response to what the text says.

SBSG material varies, but most churches use open-ended questions to cause participants to reflect and respond to the material. Some churches used icebreaker-type questions just to get people interacting. Multiple-choice questions are sometimes helpful to break up the routine. However, strategic open-ended questions make participants wrestle with the text or big idea in a way the pastor hopes they will respond during the week after he preaches. Some models provide a prayer prompt or opportunity in the group that is related to the message. Some also use a memory verse to reinforce the sermon and small-group discussion.

OVERCOMING THE CHALLENGES

The SBSG model for discipleship has challenges that can be overcome with good strategy and sensitivity in decision making. The survey churches identified six challenges connected to the SBSG model. Below are the six challenges and recommendations on how to overcome them.

Challenge #1: The Time Factor

Pastors and ministers who use the SBSG model will find it difficult to carve out time to develop the material. A busy, complex world keeps ministers busy. Sermon preparation can be a challenge. How can a preacher find time to add small-group question development to his schedule? The way to overcome the challenge of time is through time management. Planning ahead at least twice a year for ten weeks of preaching would make the task more manageable. Using a template of questions that are the same every week is another method of easing preparation of small-group questions. If a preaching team is used, rotate the preparation of the SBSG questions to the one not preaching. A small-church pastor could share the question writing with a team, a writer in the congregation, or a spouse. The bottom line is if the SBSG model is important, leaders will make time to prepare for it.

Challenge #2: Repetition

One of the complaints against the SBSG model is that it is repetitious. People do not always like studying the same topic as the Sunday sermon. One way to overcome repetition is by changing the paradigm. Pastors need to get people to buy in to the idea that relationship building is the main purpose of the SBSG. Second, material needs to be an extension of the Sunday sermon, not a regurgitation of the sermon. Participants need to know they are learning something new on the same topic. A misunderstanding when it comes to using the SBSG model is that the model allows no relief for variety. The model can be used for seasons of time, not necessarily year-round. This allows groups to use other studies to meet felt needs within the group. Momentum and unity that come from using the SBSG approach can provide motivation for participants to overlook repetition.

Challenge #3: Developing a Writing Team

The development of a good writing team can be a challenge worth overcoming. This challenge initially involves recruiting and keeping good writers. For some small churches the challenge is not having people in the church who are published writers. There are usually a few people who can write well and need only to catch the vision of writing SBSG material. Two or three volunteers with the right vision casting and training can become a great writing team.

Another option is to use professional writers from within the congregation. Larger churches will probably have a few writers who could be recruited as volunteers; or if budget funds are available, they could be paid. Churches that take writer recruitment and development seriously put money into the challenge. They send the team or a leader to a writing seminar or conference. Skilled authors will enjoy the opportunity to use their giftedness. They could also be asked to recruit apprentices to train to expand the writing team.

Another option is to have the staff write the material as a part of the weekly or monthly staff meeting. This can happen in collaboration. It can also happen in partial collaboration with the educational or spiritual formation pastor being responsible for final development.

Challenge #4: Felt-Need Studies

Offering felt needs or specialty studies is a challenge to the SBSG model. This challenge will come in the form of people or groups stating they need to deal with a felt-need study. This could be a study on stewardship or marriage issues, for example. Whatever the felt-need request, the SBSG model allows for it. While the SBSG material is the preferred material, small groups should be allowed to take time away from the SBSG material to meet felt needs and break up the monotony. Allowing this once a year could be a good way to give small groups a sense of ownership.

Challenge #5: Informational vs. Process Approach

Getting church members to make the paradigm shift from informational, university-model types of education to process, a relational type of education, is difficult. The principle of relationship building as a priority over information and content is not easy for the Western cultural mind-set. The way to make this shift in thinking is to get people to see the value of relationship building. They need to realize people need friends as well as information. This challenge can be overcome, but it will take sensitivity. The limits of informational programs need to be exposed. This exposure needs to show that programs dispense information but leave out relationship building. Programs do not need to be belittled. They only need to be expanded.

Jesus's method of growing his followers is an excellent way to get church members to embrace the SBSG model. It is difficult for people to argue against the need to build relationships. Jesus spent time with his followers, and in the process of doing life with them, he taught them. Showing people the model Jesus used to provide balance between the informational, programmatic model and the relational model will help church members embrace the SBSG model. People need to understand that information and content are not being watered down or downgraded. Pairing people with mature Christians in small groups centered on the content from the sermon will provide an atmosphere for transformation.

Challenge #5: Getting Total Participation

Getting everyone to use the SBSG process is a challenge. The way to solve this challenge is to change the requirement. None of the SBSG churches expected total participation from the congregation. There are always people who will not participate in a small group. Some will just not embrace the SBSG model, especially those in churches where the structure is set up with another established model. SBSG churches should set up an atmosphere of expectation of small-group participation by all members. This expectation should not be a requirement. It can be a godly expectation communicated with encouragement.

CHANGE UP YOUR GAME

The SBSG model for discipleship is working in many churches. The model should be considered as an option by any culturally sensitive church desiring to make disciples in a simple, comprehensive way. The SBSG model is new. There is not much in print about the model. George Barna suggested the SBSG model as a possible way to make disciples. He affirmed how material "related to the sermon"[102] could be reinforced with content-heavy teaching in large groups and applied in discussion in small groups.[103] Willow Creek Community Church found the SBSG model effective in moving new believers across the spectrum of Christian growth. New believers become more Christ-centered because Willow Creek realized, "We need to extend the impact of our weekend services."[104] Since 2009, SBSG use has exploded. Most new church plants are using the approach for all the reasons stated. If our church plants are using the model, then why should you not use it? What if the SBSG approach actually provided the structure and unity needed for produce renewal and momentum in your church?

KEY QUESTIONS

1. The authors write, "A sense of connectedness around the Word of God that produces ministry and missions is what seems to be missing." Is this true in your church? What is causing the disconnect?

2. What appeals to you about sermon-based small groups? What would be the pluses for your congregation? What problems would this plan solve?

3. What does a sermon-based small-groups plan demand of a pastor? What does it demand of others?

4. Considering the characteristics of the sermon-based small-groups model, which would be the greatest challenge in your church? How can you overcome the challenge(s)?

5. What are the benefits of this discipleship process in your church?

CONCLUSION

We earnestly believe the process of revitalization begins in the gospel of Jesus Christ. This is what spiritual renewal is about, the people of God returning to the Word of God, hearing from God, and obeying God. When a pastor emphasizes the gospel the church benefits from the impact of Scripture.

As we have researched, implemented, and evaluated church-revitalization methods, we believe a church focusing on a method of sermon-based approaches accomplishes a greater impact while redeeming the pastor's time. The distractions of pastoring a church are numerous. Add to that the necessity to rightly presenting the Word of God to the congregation, and a pastor has a massive undertaking. In traditional churches pastors are preaching two, three, or even four times a week on different topics. Pastors get creative in their approaches, but the reality is, they are focused on multiple messages for the congregation. Most pastors spend 70 percent or more of their time on the Sunday morning message. Meaning the other times the Word is opened do not receive as much preparation. The method we are encouraging in this writing strategically allows the pastor not only to reinforce his Sunday morning sermon but also to dig deeper and explore more with his congregation. We believe this is the missing element in the disciple-making process. If a pastor has prayed through the most important message to deliver for the week, this message needs to be reinforced.

A simple four- to six-week series on prayer, or renewal, or principles of revitalization can make all the difference in getting your church jump-started if things are plateaued. Our approach here is simple, short, creates community, creates team, and leverages the Word or God. The hardest part of doing this approach to start revitalization of the church you serve will be found in your group leaders. Yet, if you pray now and get a few key leaders on board with the possibilities, it can work for you. Introduce the idea to your staff. Get leaders involved in the planning! Set a date to do a four week series six months out. Create momentum. The effort and journey alone will give motivation to your church context. If you start early and prayerful, planning for Great Commission success, then you will get it. We often tell people, "If you want Great Commission results, focus on Great Commission tasks."

KEY QUESTIONS

1. How has this book changed your view of church revitalization?

2. Outline your plan for making revitalization changes in your church.

3. If you were going to pick a month to do a four-week series on revitalizing prayer, which month would it be?

4. Could you get your leaders, on board to agree to do a church wide, four-week series based on this plan? Preach a series on prayer and then reinforce it with sermon based small groups?

REMEMBER THE PRAYERS!

Here's a way to start the revitalization process:

Step #1. Evaluate your prayer culture.

Grade it. Keep it simple. Do not make excuses. Acknowledge the praying that is happening, but do not make it bigger than it is. Evaluate your leaders. Are Acts 6:4 and 4:31 priorities in your church?

Step #2. Study what Scriptures.

Review and personalize what the New Testament says about how a church should be praying.

Step #3. Make a short implementation list.

You probably have prayer dreams in your heart and head. Get them on a napkin, whiteboard, or note-taking pad. Look at what you can get done. Ask the Lord to give you timing for implementing.

Step #4. Identify an initial group.

Identify twenty-four people you know will pray. Begin praying for these people.

Step#5. Create a "boiler room."

Host a prayer and pie evening at your home. Tell this story:

> Five young college students were spending a Sunday in London, so they went to hear the famed C. H. Spurgeon preach. While waiting for the doors to open, the students were greeted by a man who said, "Gentlemen, let me show you around. Would you like to see the heating plant of this church?" They were not particularly interested, for it was a hot day in July. But they didn't want to offend the stranger, so they consented. The young men were taken down a stairway, a door was quietly opened, and their guide whispered, "This is our heating plant." Surprised, the students saw seven hundred people bowed in prayer, seeking a blessing on the service that was soon to begin in the auditorium above. Softly closing the door, the gentleman then introduced himself. It was none other than Charles Spurgeon.[105]

Explain the need for prayer in the church. Give each participant a four-by-six-inch card to keep in their

Bibles. On the card write "the fuel of preaching is prayer." Or "pray the Spirit will move while pastor preaches." Each week when you open your Bible in church for the sermon, put this card on your Bible at the passage." These twenty-four pray-ers are to pray for the service continually.

Step #6. Start using a prayer request card.

Begin to receive prayer requests in your morning service once a month. Give out a prayer request card. Let people fill it out during a couple of minutes during the service. Then place the cards in a box in a room designated for prayer. Get your twenty-four people to start praying through those cards. The reason for the cards is to minister to the people. You will be amazed at how this will change your prayer culture.

Step #7. Establish a prayer room.

Step #8. Utilize SBSG to reinforce your prayer strategy.

Use sermon-based small groups to reinforce a four-week series on prayer. You can use your existing small groups, or you can create short-term small groups for the series duration only. We suggest off-campus options. The staff, elders, or deacons and other leaders could create prayer groups for four weeks. Refresh yourself on Jeremiah Lanphier's strategy for praying during the 1857 prayer revival. When you start the series on prayer (or other topics in revitalization), use these sermon-based groups to undergird the movement in prayer.

Step #9. Create a prayer opportunity for pastors in your circle.

Step #10. Cast vision with your leaders.

Communicate to your leaders that staying where you are in praying is not an option and what will happen when the church prays.

ABOUT THE AUTHORS

Kenneth Priest (DEdMin, Midwestern Baptist Theological Seminary) serves as the Director of Convention Strategies for the Southern Baptists of Texas Convention, as an adjunct professor with Midwestern Baptist Theological Seminary and Southwestern Baptist Theological Seminary, and as the interim director for the Center for Church Revitalization with SWBTS. Kenneth is married to Debbi.

Alan Stoddard (DMin, Gordon Conwell Theological Seminary) serves as a senior pastor in New Mexico. Alan has served churches across the Southwest in roles of evangelism, executive pastor, senior pastor, and co-pastor. Alan is married to Jeana and they have one daughter.

NOTES

Introduction

[1] Ken Hemphill, *Connected Community: Becoming Family through Church*, (Tigerville, SC: Auxano Press, 2013), 10.

[2] Thomas T. Clegg and Warren Bird, *Lost in America: How You and Your Church Can Impact the World Next Door* (Loveland, CO: Group Publishing, 2001), 27.

[3] David Olson, *The American Church in Crisis* (Grand Rapids, MI: Zondervan, 2008), 17.

[4] Ibid., 17–18.

[5] "Hemphill: Revitalizing Churches Entails Sunday School Strategy," *Baptist Press*, April 21, 1998, accessed May 25, 2013, http://www.bpnews.net/bpnews.asp?id=2199.

[6] Clegg and Bird, *Lost in America*, 25.

[7] Ibid., 33.

[8] Olson, *The American Church in Crisis*, 36.

[9] Ibid., 29.

[10] *Southern Baptist Directory Services*, accessed October 25, 2013, http://sbds.lifeway.com.

[11] Clegg and Bird, *Lost in America*, 25.

[12] Ibid., 36.

[13] Olson, *The American Church in Crisis*, 15.

Chapter 1: A Biblical Case for Church Revitalization

[14] "revitalize," *Merriam-Webster.com.* ccessed September 6, 2019, https://www.merriam-webster.com/dictionary/revitalize.

15 John Nolland, *The Gospel of Matthew: a Commentary on the Greek Text*, New International Greek Testament Commentary (Grand Rapids, MI: Eerdmans, 2005; Carlisle: Paternoster Press, 2005), 1265.

16 Stuart K. Weber, *Matthew*, vol. 1, Holman New Testament Commentary (Nashville, TN: B&H, 2000), 484.

17 Craig Blomberg, *Matthew*, vol. 22, The New American Commentary (Nashville: B&H, 1992), 431.

18 Nolland, "Preface."

19 Blomberg, *Matthew*, 431.

20 Weber, *Matthew*, 484.

21 Ibid., 485.

22 Nolland, 1270.

23 Weber, *Matthew*, 485.

24 Nolland, 1265–66.

25 John B. Polhill, *Acts*, vol. 26, The New American Commentary (Nashville: B&H, 1995), 84.

26 Ibid., 86.

27 Kenneth O. Gangel, *Acts*, vol. 5, Holman New Testament Commentary (Nashville, TN: B&H, 1998), 11.

28 Polhill, *Acts*, 121.

29 Gangel, *Acts*, 32.

30 Polhill, *Acts*, 121.

31 Ibid., 121–22.

32 Gangel, *Acts*, 32.

33 Ibid.

34 W. Robertson Nicoll, *The Expositor's Greek Testament: Commentary*, vol. 2 (New York: George H. Doran Company, n.d.), 98.

35 Kendell H. Easley, *Revelation*, vol. 12, Holman New Testament Commentary (Nashville, TN: B&H, 1998), 34.

36 Colin J. Hemer, *The Letters to the Seven Churches of Asia in Their Local Setting* (Grand Rapids, MI: Eerdmans, 1989), 39.

37 John F. Walvoord, "Revelation," ed. J. F. Walvoord and R. B. Zuck, *The Bible Knowledge Commentary: An Exposition of the Scriptures* (Wheaton, IL: Victor Books, 1985), 933.

38 G. K. Beale, *The Book of Revelation: a Commentary on the Greek Text*, New International Greek Testament Commentary (Grand Rapids, MI: Eerdmans, 1999; Carlisle, Cumbria: Paternoster Press, 1999), 228–29.

39 Beale, *The Book of Revelation*, 229.

40 Easley, *Revelation*, 34.

41 Ibid., 35.

42 Beale, *The Book of Revelation*, 229.

43 Ibid., 230.

44 F. L. Cross and Elizabeth A. Livingstone, *The Oxford Dictionary of the Christian Church* (Oxford; New York: Oxford University Press, 2005), 1393.

45 Easley, *Revelation*, 35.

46 Ibid.

47 Beale, *The Book of Revelation*, 233.

48 Hemer, *The Letters to the Seven Churches of Asia in Their Local Setting*, 42.

49 Easley, *Revelation*, 36.

50 John Peter Lange, Philip Schaff, et al., *A Commentary on the Holy Scriptures: Nehemiah* (Bellingham, WA: Logos Bible Software, 2008), 35.

51 Mervin Breneman, *Ezra, Nehemiah, Esther*, vol. 10, electronic ed., The New American Commentary (Nashville: B&H, 1993), 224.

52 Ibid.

53 Ibid.

54 Lange, Schaff, et al., *A Commentary on the Holy Scriptures: Nehemiah*, 35.

55 Breneman, *Ezra, Nehemiah, Esther*, 224.

56 Ibid., 225.

57 Ibid.

58 Ibid.

59 Ibid.

60 Blomberg, *Matthew*, 431.

Chapter 2: On the Role of the Pastor and Small Groups

61 Gene Getz, *Elders and Leaders: God's Plan for Leading the Church* (Chicago: Moody, 2003), 185.

62 Robert E. Coleman, *The Master Plan of Evangelism* (Grand Rapids: Revell, 1993), 21.

63 Getz, *Elders and Leaders*, 56.

64 Ibid., 42. Acts 11:30 is the first mention of elders in the New Testament.

65 Alexander Strauch, *Biblical Eldership: Restoring the Eldership to Its Rightful Place in the Church* (Littleton, CO: Lewis and Roth Publishers, 1997), 40.

[66] The apostle Paul often ended his letters with a by-name greeting to those whom he had mentored and developed or who also had helped him in the missionary journeys.

[67] Getz, *Elders and Leaders*, 181.

[68] Ibid., 219.

[69] Ibid.

[70] Ibid., 222.

[71] Fancis Foulkes, "Ephesians: An Introduction and Commentary," *Tyndale New Testament Commentary* (Grand Rapids: Eerdmans, 1968), 119.

[72] There is a strong consensus in the academic community that the roles of "pastor" and "teacher" in Ephesians 4:11 should be understood as linked with one another. As such, we assume that these two terms comprise one position–"pastor-teacher."

[73] *The American Heritage Dictionary of the English Language*, Dictionary.com, 4th ed. Houghton Mifflin Company, 2004. s.v. "character," accessed November 12, 2007, http://dictionary.reference.com/browse/character.

[74] Getz, *Elders and Leaders: God's Plan for Leading the Church*, 96.

[75] John F. Walvoord, Roy B. Zuck, and Dallas Theological Seminary, *The Bible Knowledge Commentary: An Exposition of the Scriptures* (Wheaton, IL: Victor Books, 1985), 2:736.

[76] The Titus list has been arranged to align with the Timothy list so the duplicating traits are easier to identify.

[77] This list provides non-duplicating traits.

[78] Warren W. Wiersbe, *The Bible Exposition Commentary*, electronic ed., An Exposition of the New Testament Comprising the Entire 'BE' Series (Wheaton: Victor Books, 1996), 1 Timothy 3:1.

79 Thomas D. Lea and Hayne P. Griffin, *1, 2 Timothy, Titus*, electronic ed., vol. 34 of The New American Commentary (Nashville: B&H, 2001), 106.

80 Strauch, *Biblical Eldership*, 124–25.

81 Ibid., 148.

82 Ibid., 149.

83 John Franklin, *And the Place Was Shaken: How to Lead a Powerful Prayer Meeting* (Nashville: B&H, 2005), 8–9.

84 Ibid.

85 Ibid., 8.

86 Robinson, *Biblical Preaching: The Development and Delivery of Expository Messages* (Grand Rapids: Baker Academic, 2014), 107.

87 Coleman, *The Master Plan of Evangelism*, 28.

88 Ibid.

89 Ibid., 35.

90 Stuart Wright, Kirk Hadaway, and Francis Dubose, *Home Cell Groups and House Churches* (Nashville: Baptist Sunday School Board, 1987), 41.

91 Rad Zdero, *The Global House Church Movement* (Pasadena: William Carey Library, 2004), 50–51.

92 Ibid., 69.

93 Ibid., 22.

94 Ibid., 28.

95 Ibid., 30.

96 Ibid., 33.

97 Dr. Daryl Eldridge repeatedly stated this from his ministerial experience in a small men's prayer group the author has been in for eleven years. Daryl is an expert on

small groups and educational ministry. I asked Daryl how he came to this percentage, and he state it came from years of asking pastors if they participated in a small group. Daryl is president of Rockbridge Seminary, a fully online seminary at www.rockbridgeseminary.com.

[98] A simple Internet search will reveal the compromise in each case of these pastoral leaders.

Chapter 3: The Priority of Prayer in Revitalization

[99] John Franklin, *And the Place Was Shaken: How to Lead a Powerful Prayer Meeting* (Nashville: B&H, 2005), 8–9.

Chapter 4: Connecting the Sermon to the Small Group

[100] Larry Osborne, *Sticky Church* (Grand Rapids: Zondervan, 2008), 30.

[101] Hal Mayer, *Making the Critical Connection: Combining the Best of Small-Group Dynamics with Sunday School* (Nashville: Serendipity House, 2005), 8–15.

[102] George Barna, *Growing True Disciples* (Colorado Springs: Waterbrook Press, 2001), 122.

[103] Ibid.

[104] Greg L. Hawkins and Cally Parkinson, *Reveal: Where Are You? The Answer That Will Transform Your Church* (South Barrington, IL: Willow Creek Association, 2007), 66–67.

Appendix: Remember the Prayers!

[105] *Our Daily Bread*, April 24.

Are you ready to experience **turnaround** in your church?

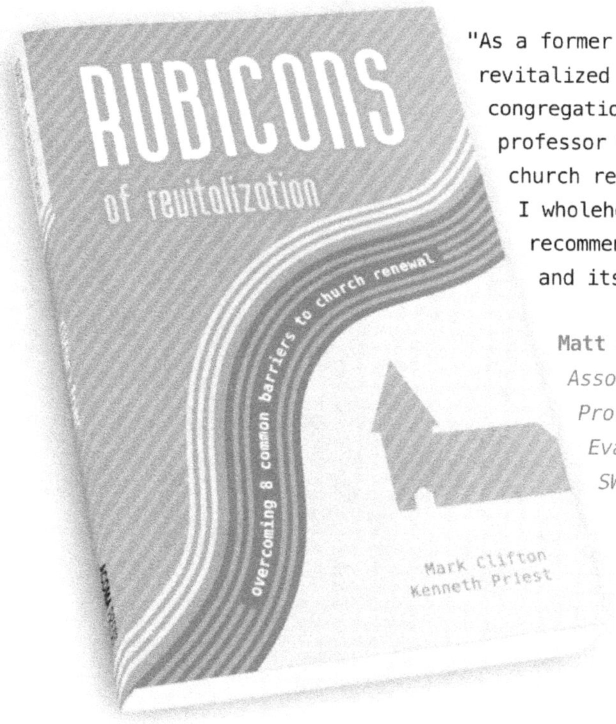

"As a former pastor who revitalized a declining congregation and now a professor who teaches church revitalization, I wholeheartedly recommend this book and its principles."

Matt Queen,
Associate Professor of Evangelism; SWBTS

RUBICONS
of revitalization

"I COMMEND THIS BOOK TO EVERY CHURCH MEMBER WHO SEEKS TO GLORIFY GOD AND EXPAND HIS KINGDOM."

- **Mark Clifton,** *National Director of Replant North American Mission Board*

This series features short, action-oriented resources aimed at equipping the North American church for a movement of church replanting, introduced by Pastor Mark Hallock's book *Replant Roadmap*.

Thousands of churches are closing their doors in United States every year in some of its fastest-growing, most under-reached neighborhoods. Yet there is much hope for these churches, particularly through the biblically-rooted, gospel-saturated work of replanting.

Designed for both group and individual study, these books will help you understand what the Bible has to say about how God builds and strengthens his church and offer you some practical steps toward revitalization in your own.

For more information, visit **acomapress.org** and **nonignorable.org**

ACOMA PRESS

Acoma Press exists to make Jesus non-ignorable by equipping and encouraging churches through gospel-centered resources.

Toward this end, each purchase of an Acoma Press resource serves to catalyze disciple-making and to equip leaders in God's Church. In fact, a portion of your purchase goes directly to funding planting and replanting efforts in North America and beyond. To see more of our current resources, visit us at *acomapress.org*.

Thank you.